THE SACRED MYSTERY MANUSCRIPTS

REVELATIONS AND INSPIRATIONS FOR YOUR SACRED FEMININE SOUL

TRICIA MARY LEE

BALBOA.
PRESS

A DIVISION OF HAY HOUSE

Artwork
Impressions of Greece and Demeter by Audrey Counsell
Fig leaf borders by Marga Felip e—Triplett

Balboa Press books may be ordered through booksellers or by contacting:

Balboa Press
A Division of Hay House
1663 Liberty Drive
Bloomington, IN 47403
www.balboapress.com.au
1-(877) 407-4847

ISBN: 978-1-4525-0349-3 (sc)
ISBN: 978-1-4525-0350-9 (e)

Printed in the United States of America

Balboa Press rev. date: 03/01/2012

I acknowledge and give thanks to
the traditional custodians of the land and Sacred culture
here in Australia.
May we all learn to respect the soul of this Sacred Earth
and live in harmony
as we create the world of our dreams.

This book is dedicated with love and gratitude to those strong and beautiful women, on Earth and in Spirit, who have taught and mothered me in my search for the truth of my feminine soul.
It is offered with eternal thanks to all
"The Gorgeous Goddess Girls."
I especially honour my spiritual lineage from
"The Olive Tree"
and give thanks to my friend and teacher, Olive Wraight.

Take this book,
Take it in the Sacred Way,
For the wisdom herein,
Will carry you home to the Beloved.

CONTENTS

YOUR INVITATION

Welcome

Women of the world, the waters are breaking, and all of us are invited to be immersed in the rebirthing of the Great Mother energy.

In preparation for this, in the auspicious year of 2000, an amazing and wonderful stream of energy started to pour forth from the Great Mother through four of her daughters, the Goddess messengers, who have been named Demeter, Ishtar, Mary, and Ceridwen.

In the form of four beautiful manuscripts, each one containing teachings to assist our spiritual realignment to the Heart of the Sacred Feminine Mystery, the Great Mother came to help us to reclaim the heart of our own personal, sacred, feminine power.

The teachings have been tried and tested in Sacred Circles of women here in West Australia and also in England.

Now it is time for these Revelations to be brought into the global domain, to be shared and used, as we here on Earth manifest the wish of the Great Mother for the rightful return of her wisdom.

This book, which contains in full *The Demeter Manuscript: The Secretas of the Great Mystery,* is the start of your Sacred Pathway to a more beautiful future for yourself, your family, your community, and our world.

Welcome and Blessed be.

A Call to All Women

The rebirth of this Great Mother Energy, being one full half of the Cosmic Life Force, which we may call Great Love, Great Spirit, Universal Energy, and other titles, is of course an event of wonderful and immensely significant dimensions.

For each and every one of us, there is a part to play.

By birthright as women, we carry on a cellular level the natural sacred soul template of the feminine half of this energy.

Your personal, sacred soul resonates and shimmers as a facet of this most magnificent, beautiful, and powerful energy of creation.

Such power.

Such privilege.

Such amazing blessings await you as you reconnect with the Natural Law of Returns that governs this way of being.

As you surrender and release any superficial notions of outer beauty, retail therapy, cosmetic appearance, false body image, and disconnected health and spirituality—you begin to prepare for the journey back home to the inner truth of

All That Is.

Each and every one of us holds the right to be a *midwife* for this time should we so choose.

By reclaiming your right to your sacred soul pathway, the Great Mother Energy can begin to rebalance the Divine Father Energy and return the Earth to balance, harmony, and great beauty so . . .

ARE YOU READY?

This is the call, which the Goddess Demeter gave in her manuscript, before she invited me, and now you personally, to begin this unique Sacred Journey to the heart of the Great Mystery.

"Ready for what?" you may ask.

Ready for change?

Ready for transformation in yourself?

And, more powerfully, for change in the way of the world and thereby the cosmos?

Ready to embrace your feminine soul, the source of your inner fragrance, the home of the Universal Sacred Feminine Soul?

These are some of the answers I am able to offer you now, having worked with Demeter myself and with groups of other beautiful women over the last eleven years since she gave her teachings, in that auspicious start to our millennium, the year 2000.

But specifically, and most importantly I feel, it is to be ready for yourself to grow into your own true beauty and power.

You see, she goes onto explain that once you have taken this journey of deep soul discovery and learning, then your whole life, your way of being you, will be transformed and you will never be the same again.

This I can vouch for.

Think well on this, for, as she tells us later, we always have a choice.

Again Demeter asks, "Are you sure you are ready?" before she explains a little more of the journey to the Great Mystery over the threshold of that which she calls "the knowingness of the heart".

She goes on to tell us that the Great Mystery is the term that we use to represent *"All That Is"* and that we are not to confuse it with our limited notions of *God* because we have been living in a cloud of misunderstanding.

With a third time of asking, "So, my friends, are you ready?" and a third chance for your affirmation, she welcomes you to step through the portals of these pages for your journey home to *"All That Is."*

> ***So, my beautiful women of the Earth,***
> ***When you are ready,***
> ***Be***
> ***Welcome Home.***

Saying "Yes" to Your Personal Transformation

If you feel you are now ready to say "Yes", then maybe I can add a little personal information from my experience, which will help you understand and prepare for this journey of inner transformation.

I feel that then I have helped Demeter.

It can seem a bit daunting, a bit like stepping into the unknown to say "Yes" to a journey where you have no clear picture of the destination.

How can you truly know your inner landscape if you have not had the time or space, or inclination, to journey there?

So first of all, I feel you need to recognise and honour yourself as a seeker, a being of courage, a woman of quest.

It may be that your journey so far has opened some of the doors, which are already challenging the *orthodox* way of being.

You may be working with natural health, spirituality, personal growth and development, or what is considered "new wave" thinking.

For each of you however, there are simple core requirements that help to ensure that you are in the right space at the right time for your best outcome.

Time and Commitment

What I feel you need for the Demeter pathway is the ability to commit to yourself the time and love that you will need to thoroughly take the teachings from each Secreta and make it your own.

This is often a very hard thing for a busy mother, woman, wife, career woman, artist or carer to allow for herself.

It is so easy to make time to take the kids to sport, to organize for your ageing parents, to produce the necessary round of family meals, to fulfil the work expectations, and so on ad infinitum, over and above honouring our inner callings.

But it is necessary to make time.

It is absolutely vital.

This is all about you.

Initially this is a time each month of at least two hours to simply read and reflect on the Secreta for that month, plus extra time over the month to act upon it and let yourself be guided to consider changes and new ways of being you.

I suggest that you keep a journal to write, draw, and document your efforts at Soul Gardening and your discoveries as you dig deeper on a soul level.

Demeter also gives some *homework!*

So you will need time to practise each new skill and also some time to play creatively as you discover the jewels of your inner landscape.

As with any learning journey, the more you put in, the more you will see return to yourself.

If you are working with the *Sacred Journal: Soul Gardening with Demeter,* which is included in this edition, then there are many more suggestions and ideas for activities to support you.

If you are forming or are part of a group, a sacred circle, then there will need to be a consensus on the group time as well as a personal commitment to *homework.*

Your commitment is a measure of the value you place on your own sacred soul self.

Honesty and Courage

The nature of any new gardening project is that we first have to look honestly at what we have got, explore what may be underneath, and then add fertilizer so that we can plant what we have chosen to grow.

On a metaphysical level, this means we will be digging up any buried *weeds* and recycling them.

We will also be finding the jewels within.

It can bring forth tears and laughter. Our emotions have to connect with our mind in order for the soul to be engaged, but we are women so this is nothing new for us, or is it?

What often reveals itself is a buried sense of poor, inadequate, or inappropriate emotional mothering, which is linked to our Earth, birth mothers.

Where our mothers have pursued an academic pathway or worked full time, where our mothers have done it tough on the land, where our mothers have been subjugated to the male ascendancy, then we may be surprised to discover a sense of grief or emotional lack at something we feel we have missed. It could even manifest as resentment and conflict with our own feminine self.

The tenderness and mothering wisdom which we discover from Demeter helps us rediscover what we have lost, what we have been unconsciously searching for, in our roles as modern women.

It takes honesty and courage to look at this and other issues, but it is of primary importance for our sacred feminine soul.

This is bigger than our personal agendas.

It is deeply connected with the global suppression of the true feminine, matriarchal energy and power that have resulted from patriarchal social, cultural, political, economic, and religious organizations.

Our education and partnership in the workforce have been a huge step forward in the emancipation debate of last century, but, for many of us, it has isolated us emotionally and placed us in competition with each other when our natural way is to thrive on co-operation.

You can see that there is still more work for us to be accepted equally for the natural way that is powerful for women.

Finally, it seems, the last *shackle* is being challenged, as we are helped to reclaim our right to feminine spiritual wisdom.

When we join together in our sacred feminine souls, we gradually and gently put in place the final piece of our emancipation.

It requires women of honesty and courage.

That is you.

Humour and Respect

Demeter has a lovely sense of humour and it is certainly a great asset for this work.

When we distance ourselves from our ego selves, then the humour of being a woman arises spontaneously.

It is a great coping strategy for we are being presented with some major challenges globally as well as personally, and it helps to keep a perspective on our role in all of this.

The clearing of our biblical legacy of guilt is a primary step forward as Demeter helps us to move into a situation of full respect and gratitude for who we truly are, for everything we have had to cope with, and for all the lessons we have already learnt.

Within Sacred Circle, these qualities grow in abundance and enrich our whole sense of value for womanhood today.

I have never been anything other than totally impressed and overwhelmed at the resilience and coping strategies of all the women in my groups. They enrich me in a way I cannot describe, but I am certainly proud to be amongst them.

Humour and respect are two qualities you can grow, two blessings you can receive, as you give yourself permission to commit to this pathway of the sacred feminine.

Self Love

In my first little book, *Stop Punishing Yourself,* I explored many ways in which we simply devalue ourselves by our ways of thinking.

I used the metaphor of a spell from a wicked witch, as sometimes it seems like our self-sabotage is from an endless well of self-esteem that is programmed negative and often destructive.

As we become conscious of our true soul templates, we can finally begin to challenge the stereotypes and assumptions of the world in which we find ourselves. We can question the values that we have been raised with and become conscious of the factors influencing our decisions and choices in a fast, consumer-driven world of commerce and technology.

It is not always a world that appreciates our finer feminine qualities of tenderness, beauty, creativity, intuition, sensitivity, cooperation, and good natural health.

First then, we have to value and appreciate ourselves, and then each other.

We have to learn what it means to live with an open heart and be soul driven.

We have to learn to love and honour our innate gifts of the Sacred Feminine.

Then, and only then, can the Cosmic Sacred Feminine Soul energy be brought back and fully into balance.

Our self-love on this soul level is unconditional, is eternal, and is the power that lifts us upwards.

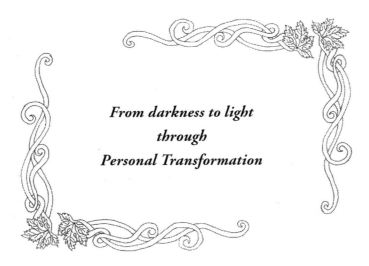

From darkness to light
through
Personal Transformation

The Arrival of the Sacred Mystery Manuscripts

In order to describe the arrival of these manuscripts, I will try to explain the mystery that we cannot logically understand, that which is unseen and falls into what we may call an act of faith.

I myself consider them to be a great gift, in the way of a miracle, but I am unable to give a definition or rational analysis of how they came about, only what I felt and experienced as I was transformed into a "scribe" for beings that are not with us in body, on this physical plane of being.

Some call it channelling, clairaudience, claircognisance, or mediumship; others call it the way of the mystic or prophet. I have dwelt on this and have certainly wrestled with my own conscience and faith.

Maybe in today's technology it can be simply compared to a download.

I now believe the name is really of no consequence as the teachings themselves have proved to be the vital link which touches and transforms each woman who commits to the journey, each and every gentle step of the way.

However, for any others who feel that this way of the scribe, to document the *downloads* from an unseen source, is a pathway they want to commence, then I will share something of the process, as self-doubt can be a great obstacle to the gifts of Spirit and Great Beauty.

Usually my routine for this work would be to set a regular time when I would show up at my kitchen table with a pen and paper. Always I would light a candle and some incense and ask for the intentions of Great Love to be made manifest in whatever answer, message or words of wisdom that came forth. In this way, I had been receiving answers to some deep and personal questions which always seemed to provide a different and much more enlightened angle on the actual issues than my human brain seemed capable of finding. I can recommend this way of discovering spiritual insight for anyone with a sincere wish for self-realisation. Closing with a thanks and a

blessing for the energy source is as important and just as appreciated as in any situation where insight or advice is sought from a wiser friend.

It s also important to drink plenty of water and to remember that your energy resonance is affected by your health and well-being, so do not try this if you are tired or unwell.

Demeter, however, was a very different process when she arrived in 2000.

It is significant (although of course I have only realised this as I now look back and can see the full circle of events) that I had just been blessed to move to Broome in the tropical far north Kimberley region of Western Australia.

We had visited Broome in 1989 on our first family trip to Australia from our home in England. We were travelling by overnight coach from visiting our family in Darwin, in the Northern Territory, down the west coast to our final destination of Perth.

In the warm, velvet darkness of night, as the coach stopped for the smokers in the middle of nowhere, I got off the coach to feel the warm night air. And I remember a breathtaking sense of magic. There were small fires burning across the landscape and something stirred in my soul, something called me, but I had no idea what. I was thirty-seven years old and still searching.

Breaking the journey for a couple of days, at this small remote township called Broome, which is famous for its pearls, we soaked up the magical atmosphere of the long, golden beach, the spectacular sunsets, the diverse and multicultural aspects of the history, the Chinatown, and the raw red Earth set against the turquoise ocean.

In a spontaneous act of almost reverent worship and deep symbolic connection, but without realising its awesome power, I scooped up some of the magnificent red Earth and later put it into a special box that I had bought and I took it back home to England.

Little did I imagine that three years later we would be migrating to Australia, and in a further eight years we ourselves would be living right there in the heart of Broome. (Moral of this story: take great care with your symbolic actions!)

Another example of what seemed like conspiracy/coincidence by the universal energy occurred then in our miraculous move to Broome.

In order to move from the country town where we had been living and working for the last seven years, we had to apply for transfer. I wanted to head to the south west coast and so our transfer list had a town called Albany as our first choice, with Broome as the last preference.

Curiously (or not!), the fax to the education department did not send on the first time and so my husband, John, had to resend it. Without my knowledge, he decided to change the order of our choices, putting Broome at the top of the list. Amazingly, we were then granted our first choice and so we ended up in Broome! It was considered a prize to be given work there; it was literally held to be a case of stepping into *dead men's shoes!*

I was initially angry that he had changed the list without consulting me first, but, all the same, it felt like we had won Lotto!

Some simply called it a ticket to paradise.

Broome is a unique place with a very strong indigenous energy and home to one of the world's best beaches; it is a powerful place of high resonance and great natural beauty. It flourishes with the arts and artists.

In the dry season, there is a fabulous celebration that honours The Staircase to the Moon, a stunning visual event where the rising full moon creates a virtual staircase as it shimmers over the horizon across the waters of Roebuck Bay.

It's not surprising then that it provides inspiration to the soul, with openings for spiritual growth and a potential doorway to sacred connections for many of the people who are drawn to visit there.

Here, the sacred is almost tangible because it is still respected and nurtured by the traditional Aboriginal owners of the land. I give thanks to them and honour the huge influence that this beautiful sacred space has had on me.

I sensed all this very deeply, but still I was totally unprepared for what this would mean for me personally as I opened to the energy like a lotus flower opening to the sun.

Before I moved up north, I had been working as a scribe for a circle of Wise Women in spirit (see my manuscript *Wise Women Words)* who had started with these beautiful but simple words of guidance:

> *Wise Women,*
> *Come together*
> *Your strength is as one*
> *Be as jewels*
> *Clear and Bright*
> *Rare and precious beauty*
> *In the darkest night*
> *Hearts of Love*
> *Be pure*
> *Be true*
> *Shining light*
> *Shining Light*

I see now how this was a preparation for the work that was yet to come, but at the time I simply wrote the one-off beautiful inspirations, as they were given, and shared them where I could.

Curiously, they were all focused on women!

However, since the upheaval of moving up north, I had taken a break from my healing and women's work and was now back teaching full time, so it left little time for anything else.

Effectively, I had also stopped my regular time of "tune-in" to spirit. (A regular time commitment is considered necessary for this work as a scribe, as it is for any other kind of work!)

Of course, I was soon to learn that where there was "work" to do, I would be made fully aware. And sure enough, one day my sense of resonance started to rise as I was "tested" to receive a new resonance for this "download" of information to arrive.

Physically, it felt like I was starting a running cold with a fever but I had no other symptoms and so I carried on relaxing beside the pool as fortunately it was during the September school break.

I was given a "trial run" of information which I had to accurately repeat. It made no sense to me whatsoever and I can remember none of it now, but apparently it must have scored a "pass."

The next morning at 3:00 a.m., I awoke and felt I simply had to go to the computer and type. Normally I hand-scribe and then type, so this was very different for me.

The computer cranked up first time (not always a given in the tropics!) and I started typing.

"The Secretas of the Great Mystery" came out as the title.

I waited and thought, *An introduction would be nice.*

Sure enough, a page of explanation was given and then the title: "The First Secreta".

Off we went through the first of the "Secretas" that were to form the manuscript.

When we had finished, I wanted to acknowledge the source and so I asked for a name and was given a sense of "Dimetra."

Never heard of this name, I thought, wondering if there was a connection with Metatron for whom I had scribed a message since arriving in Broome.

Certainly, I felt it to be an ancient sacred source, but I was totally unsure from which context or culture.

I switched off the computer and went back to bed, sleeping soundly.

Next morning, I checked in my mythology book for any information on Metatron and found a reference for Demeter, Goddess from Ancient Greece.

Whoa!

As I read more, I felt totally humbled, overwhelmed, doubting myself to be good enough to be the scribe for this sacred source.

Later I went to the library and discovered her connection with the Mysteries at Eleusis which for me reassured and validated the whole process. (See later in *The Demeter Story* for this fascinating information.)

However, I was mindful of the test that I had been given and was anxious to stay clear in order to scribe without any pre—information. So I read no more.

As I reflected on the name, my old school Latin came forward and explained the meaning to be "of or from the mother." It's a generic name for a Goddess who comes as a messenger from the Universal or Cosmic Mother.

That afternoon I sat down again and Demeter gave me the "Second Secreta."

My *fever and running cold* had cleared completely!

However, I was clearly conscious that my vibrational energy was tuned very high.

As I again lay relaxing, dozing in and out of a semi-dream state, I could feel Demeter "talking" to me, urging me on, telling me that these Secretas (I realised that the additional *a* denotes the feminine in several European languages and *secret* is akin to *sacred* in the Latin root of the word) were intended to create the correct balance between men and women, that Gods, prophets, and gurus all were from the Great Mystery. But it was time for a personal relationship to be re-established in rightness, outside the establishment boundaries.

I felt excited, nervous, and overwhelmed by apprehension.

Could I do this task?

Dare I believe I was able?

Such a privilege.

Next morning, I again awoke at 3:00 a.m. and, unable to "down vibrate", got up and decided to continue.

The computer would not crank up, so I started to hand-write "The Third Secreta." My anxiety, however, was shadowing me, and I found it impossible to trust myself to be a clear and accurate scribe.

I left it halfway through and made a cup of peppermint tea, sat in reflection, and went back to bed.

When I got up the next morning, I completed the Third Secreta, again by hand, and then the computer started!

I got the distinct feeling that this was not meant to be an ordeal for me, that I should trust myself and enjoy the friendship with Demeter.

That same morning, we flowed through the Fourth Secreta and I was allowed to see how anxious Demeter was that she also should do a good job.

What a perfect partner.

I finally began to relax and appreciate her gifts, her humour, and her wisdom. She began to feel like a friend, a very dear and caring guide who was entrusting me to fulfil this role of scribe for her.

In all the work I have done for her, I have been richly rewarded with abundant energy and clarity of vision.

She has repaid me many times for the time and effort I have given for her use, both personally and in groups with other women.

I consider myself truly blessed in this friendship.

I believe it came as no coincidence that she chose her time to communicate with me during the Olympic Games, which were being held here in Sydney, Australia.

As I watched the Greek Goddess dance in the closing ceremony, announcing the next games to be in Athens, I was brought to deep tears and a special closeness for this friend I could not see.

My faith in her identity was complete.

***May her Blessings enrich your life and bring you closer to your soul destiny
within the Great Mystery as you enter into her Initiation.***

Initially I felt that The Demeter Manuscript was a one-off project, as the thirteen lessons, one for
each moon of a full calendar year, seemed to form a complete whole. But then the following year,
2001, around the same time towards the end of September, I was given The Ishtar Manuscript,
"The Jewels of The Night," to scribe.

Ishtar, I discovered, was a Goddess in ancient Sumeria.

She was a very different energy to "download" and caused me a great deal of anxiety, as she used
a much higher resonance.

Because of this, I have actually left my own responses in the text, as I searched to understand her
beautiful messages, a real affirmation of my own naivety as far as opening to the etheric gifts of
which she speaks.

Again I felt a sense of completion when the manuscript closed, but then, lo and behold, in August
2002 along came Mary of the Pure and Shining Heart with her transformational "Lessons for a
Pure and Blessed Life."

This manuscript has stood alone, in some senses, for those familiar with the Christian faith, and
she has touched many hearts on this pathway.

It does, though, form a part of the cycle that was emerging and that I share later in the Cycle of
Learning and Growth.

At the end of 2002, however, because of family concerns, we decided to move from Broome to
the Southern Forest region of West Australia, and with this, I felt my ability to work as a scribe
diminishing as my energy was consumed with the practical realities of a healing crisis within my
own family.

But there was one more manuscript to come, and finally, in 2003, I scribed *The Book of Ceremonies*
for Ceridwen, the Celtic Mother Goddess.

You can see now how the Great Mother has tried to inform us through four diverse energies, four messengers with four totally different forms and styles.

The wish to transform the world through personal transformation is vitally strong and clear.

Myself, I am still engaged in this transformation and recognise what feels like my own delay in finally reaching this stage of publication, as a wish to fully realise the significance of these teachings. Having waited and witnessed also the transformation in the lives of the other *Demeter girls,* I now feel confident that it is time for this sharing of these divine revelations for your sacred feminine soul.

So here, with my blessing, I offer you fully *The Demeter Manuscript.*

If this resonates with you, then seek further and follow on your journeywork with the next manuscript publications of Ishtar, Mary, and Ceridwen.

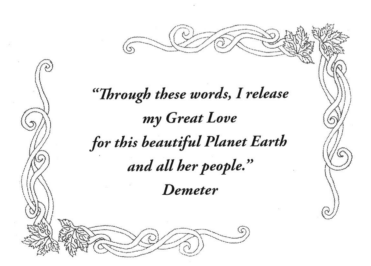

*"Through these words, I release
my Great Love
for this beautiful Planet Earth
and all her people."*
Demeter

The Demeter Manuscript

Acropolis .

AN INVITATION

You are invited to join Demeter, (Goddess of the Ancient World)
for a Sacred Journey to the Heart of the Great Mystery.

In the Ancient World, Demeter was the Goddess who gave mankind the gift of cultivation, of farming, and thus, of civilisation.

Her primary message for us today is of metaphysical cultivation, "Soul Gardening," as she calls it.

It is her wish to help us understand how each and every one of us

can live a sacred life amidst the turmoil of the modern world.

The messages are in the form of thirteen Secretas.

(The *a* ending to the root word *secret* or sacred is indicative of the feminine form in several European languages.)

The journey which she is offering to take with us will span the fullness of a year.

Naxos.

Contents

The
Secretas
of the
Great
Mystery

A voice calls from The Mystery . . .

"Are you ready?

Are you sure you are ready?

Because when you have read this, your life will never be the same again!"

Mountain Village - Naxos.

THE OPENING

*T*he *Great Mystery* is the term we use to represent *"All That Is."*

We know that in your mind space there needs to be a concrete form for all you understand.

This is the nature of the Human mind.

The Great Mystery is formless and ever moving, so do not confuse this with your limited notions of God which have been expounded by the Church.

The time is now ripe for man to understand that he has been living in a cloud of misunderstanding about "All That Is."

There are many reasons for this, and there is to be no regret, for what has been is right for what has been.

But now, such Joy is amongst those of us in Spirit who are working to increase your vision, for the telling of these Secretas will expose the fraud that you have created in limiting your mind to feel safe.

There is no danger about the Great Mystery.

It is not Witchcraft. It is not Black Magic. It is not "Definity"[that which can be defined].

This you must understand as you step over the threshold into the knowingness of the heart.

So, my friends, are you ready?

Thrice asked and thrice answered, "Yes" gives you the right to step through the portals of these pages for your journey home to All That Is.

The Great Mystery welcomes you.

THE FIRST TRIAD

THE FIRST SECRETA : TIME

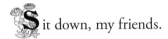it down, my friends.

Find your favourite place of quietness, for we suggest that you take this book in a sacred way: what will be revealed will lead you on a sacred journey of change, of growth, and of learning.

Therefore, do not try to cram it into a short time space between one rushed job and the next. Rather, let it linger so that you can savour the flavour.

Now, I know that your lives are incredibly busy. Amazingly zoomed up, *turbo* as you say, isn't it?

Well, this is the First Secreta: "You can change it".

As you have allowed yourself to run along with all the demands that are being placed on you, you can choose a different pace to give yourself time to breathe, to look and truly see, to listen and truly hear, to sense and truly feel, and to eat and truly taste, for in your rushing, crazy world you are forgetting that there is simple beauty which is free if only you take the time to receive it.

The pace of life is crippling you, for you are no longer able to enjoy the world in which you have chosen to live.

So take your time and linger over the simple pleasures; then you can begin to know what gives you pleasure as a reflection of part of the Great Mystery.

Even if you are working at a job which takes many hours, it is for yourself that you "come home." Be sure to give yourself a welcome, for otherwise you will not want to find your way and you will get lost.

Many people are searching for that which makes them feel at home. What is your home but the body in which you dwell? So, like the snail, you are carrying your home with you all the time.

You may need shelter, you may want food, and you may be searching for the love that you crave to make you feel good, but to feel at home you simply have to take the time to get to know yourself.

People are afraid that if they stop, they will not like what they discover about themselves.

What fools!

They are afraid that they will not like that which they have created, for their true essence is but a reflection of All That Is and is not a cause for fear but celebration.

So my friends, ponder carefully how to take your time, how to use your time, how to celebrate your time, and how to share your time with others that you may be learning in good company.

When you have taken time to reflect on all that I have said, then relax and enjoy, and then you will be ready to learn the next Secreta.

Farewell for now, *Demeter*

THE SECOND SECRETA: MONEY

Well, my good friend, now you know who I am!

This authentic understanding of the origin of this "Secreta" source is essential if women of today are to take time to listen.

So much is written and spoken that you would not want to associate with any source which was not genuine.

As you can see, I have much to share with you, and I hope you have digested lesson one!

Take your time; there is always plenty of time.

There is no need to rush, for as you see, I have waited thousands of years to bring these words of wisdom to you today.

So are we ready for our next lesson?

For these Secretas are certainly to be learnt and practised if you wish to become a Wise Woman.

Are you ready?

I hope you have drunk and eaten well.

How important it is to sustain the physical body!

As you now know, I was Goddess of the Earth and all that grows; therefore, I come to you in delight that you are enjoying the fruits of my labours.

I give you that which was revealed to me in my passage on Earth. That which I shared but which has been forgotten in the Modern World where men are holding power and women have lost their Sacred connection.

That will all be changing soon.

But not in the way of your fiery power seekers whom you would call "feminists," for they have burnt a difficult trail, but in the way of water, flow, and ease.

The revelations here will re-establish the correct balance between men and women. All will be revealed.

Are you ready?

Thrice asked and thrice answered?

Then the second Secreta awaiting you is this: "Your understanding of the role of money is too limited."

The nature of exchange is like a secret mystery in itself, for who gave one thing more value than another?

Who believed that one man was worth more than another?

Or one woman?

The value of all is equal and shall not be changed simply by man's "cost valuation."

Thus, money is acting against the better wishes of your society.

It is causing much, much trouble and there is a darkness when your people feel that they are less worthy on the basis of money and ownership.

The Secreta is that to know your own worth, you must not look outside yourself.

It is not what you have achieved materially; it is what you have learnt along the way.

It is not what you can see that "belongs" to someone else; it is how he or she shares what he or she has.

It is not always what you give away; it is in what spirit you can receive when you are in need.

These are the Sacred ways of Worth.

Can you see this, my friends?

Can you see how all has become warped in the pursuit of gold coin?

Can you feel that there is more to you than that which you can show? More than what you are owning?

This is a two part Secreta, eh?

Are you ready?

Of course you are, because you can see I know.

The next part is that when you start doing things without money, slowly, you begin to understand your true value.

I want you to think about this carefully, for I am not suggesting that you should live in poverty. That is not the way of an Abundant Goddess, but I am telling you that you can give and receive for free in some parts of your life and you will feel altogether much happier about the kind of person you are.

You are taking a *detour*, if you like; you are giving life a chance without money, and believe me that you will be surprised at your increase in value.

This will take some time to put into practise so be sure to practise well before we come to our next Secreta.

I bid you farewell till next time,

Demeter

THE THIRD SECRETA: SOUL GARDENING

Greetings, dear ones. I hope you have rested well and are sharing your gifts for free—well, some of them—for the first two Secretas may seem simple, but they are two of the hardest to practise in your world.

Always be mindful of your actions, for the trap of the world is set for power and control. You are being controlled by false powers if Time and Money are your Masters.

Let us prepare for the next Secreta.

I hope you are ready.

What is this *ready?*

Open to listen, ready to hear.

Open to see, ready to vision.

Open to sense, ready to feel.

The Secretas need ready souls, so you see it is much needed that you are ready!

The Third Secreta is the completion of the first triad. Like building blocks, this is the foundation stone.

So are we ready?

It is no use knowing how to build and wanting a new house or temple, but not putting into practise that which you have learnt. So be sure you are ready to build for yourself, for you are indeed building that which will form the foundation of your life from here on, ever forward. The work you are doing now will define that which is to come. Each one of you will be working in different ways, and this will create the right environment for that which you want to receive at your core.

Now I am sure you are ready, so relax, be comfortable, and be trusting of yourself.

Listen; the Secreta is this: "Your Soul is part of the Great Mystery."

Your Lifeblood is sacred from This Source, and when you feel this in your heart space, you will be able to use it to guide you.

Your "Soul" is as the Earth's "Soil." If it is rich and nourished, much will grow in your life, but if it is hungry and sore, abused or neglected, then it will be barren. No matter how fancy you make it look, it will not bear fruit, so be sure to nourish your Soul.

I can see that this is not an easy thing for all of you to grasp, and this is because you have confused your Soul with "God," and for many of you, "God" is a part of the religion which you have rejected. So be it.

Let it be, but work on separation and forgiveness.

Your Soul belongs to the Great Mystery, which is outside doctrine, religion, and worship.

All these things are man's attempts to give form and control to something which is beyond him.

Let them go, but accept that there was a time and a place when they were valid. Feel not bitter about this.

All is changing.

Please see it is not my wish to undermine the faith of any good person merely to give faith to those who have turned away because of the rigid controls which they sense to be wrong.

The Soul endures and is forgiving, so nurture it with kindness, gentleness, joy, happiness, and love.

Be not abusing your Soul because of man's mistakes.

Now is the time to grow.

To feel your Soul is to feel the Great Mystery at work.

Your Soul is your giftedness, your vision for truth, your wish for a better world, and your desire to contribute, so acknowledge these aspects of your self, and there you will meet the Great Mystery—in the core of your very Being.

This is not a ritual which needs pomp and circumstance or elaborate clothes and buildings. This is a connectedness which weaves daily through each moment of your life.

As your Soul grows, so too does your Life.

Is this what you want?

Remember you always have choice so if you answer "Yes," then be prepared for an abundant, flourishing tree of life.

If you answer "No," then your tree of life will be small, malnourished, and without fruit.

It is good to know you have the choice, eh?

This is the Third Secreta of the Great Mystery.

I bid you practise nurturing if you answered "Yes"—Soul Gardening!

More of this once you have started digging, and be sure to pull the weeds out by the roots!

Until we are ready next time, your loving friend,

Demeter

THE SECOND TRIAD

THE FOURTH SECRETA : FRAGRANCE AND FLAVOUR

Back so soon, you may feel that you are a slow learner, but in the history of the human race, this time dimension within which you have chosen to learn is indeed very fast.

This is a measure of your hunger, of your desire for answers to that for which you have been questing since your birth.

This Fourth Secreta is the starting point for a new dimension in your lives, that of fragrance and flavour, for these are two deep sensations which have been lost in the surge towards intellectual power.

This is not to say that there is no value in the intellect, for it is a part of the equation of the whole. However, when it flows over and subsumes those which are its partners, then it becomes like a conquering general who loses sight in battle as to the reason for the fight.

The intention, of course, is to ensure "freedom," but if the freedom that is won is then replaced with another set of rules which seek to restrict those who fought for freedom in the first place, then the intention is lost.

This is the way of the intellect today, and this has taken you further back in your understanding of the Great Mystery. The preoccupation with logic, with scientific proof, and with the need to see all that is to be believed has reduced the Sacred Mysteries to the realm of myth and legend. There is much in the workings of the universe that is beyond the tools that the intellect has yet accessed, and so I am encouraging you once more to explore that which is unseen.

In this way, you will gain the vision that you need to trust the magnificence and power of this Great Mystery.

There have been many fights for freedom in the history of humankind, and each time the hope was for a new order.

Of course, we know here in Spirit that there will be no new order until man releases his desire for personal power and control over others.

I digress, and I want to be sure that you are open and ready today for your senses to connect with my own.

This fourth secret begins a new era in your awareness, in the growth of who you are in your understanding of the infinity of the Great Mystery.

Imagine yourself walking along the shore of a distant lake. It is dusk, the aroma of the evening is seeping into your pores, and you can sense yourself as part of this fragrance, as if you were dissolving in it and it were washing right through your body to the innermost centre of your bones, to the core of your bodily organs, to the very cells of your blood. You are enchanted, the fragrance owns you, and yet it has no value but that you sense it and let it in. This is the way of life when you are nurturing your soul.

Pay attention to those things that you do in life which bring you close to a feeling of fragrance, for this is a measure of your proximity to the Great Mystery. You will begin to recognise these moments, and you will want to make them last a little longer. You will want to feel fragrance in your life each day, for it has an addictive quality.

In so doing, you are bringing yourself home to a place that is fragrant. This is an experience of great beauty. You will no longer need artificial fragrances, for you will exude a fragrance which is unique to you and which will delight all those who happen to waft through your space of being.

Do you like the idea of this fragrant space?

Please give yourself time to offload any thoughts that can act as poisons, any "toxic" feelings for yourself or others, as these will create unpleasant aromas. Soon you will be able to recognise the difference between the sweet fragrances of those who are like you in intention and those who could harm you with their thoughts and actions.

Each action has a fragrance, and you will smell that which would be sour for you. This will help you guide yourself to a place of "rightness" for your actions to be received with appreciation.

This is similar to your sense of "taste."

Let yourself savour the flavour of your life when it is sweet, when it is sour, when it is bitter, when it is pure, when it is effervescent, when it is dull, when it is sharp, and when it is soft.

The flavour of your life is in your hands, in the planting, the growing, the harvesting, the preparation, the serving, and the digesting of those seeds that you have chosen to nurture in your Soul Garden.

For the taste to be sweet, you have to plant the seeds for sweetness, as whatever seeds you sow, so surely shall you reap the harvest and taste the final cuisine.

Do you like the idea of being "chefs for life"?

There is a strong connection that you will discover between the need for food and the need for life. That you have cravings is merely an indication of your inner need for that "flavour" in your life, your desire to taste abundance of that quality which you feel is missing.

Likewise, that you have "indigestion" or allergies is an indication of where you have trouble digesting aspects of those "flavours" in your life.

You can explore this further, but for now please simply be exploring the fragrance and flavour of your own life. Is it as you would be choosing? Sense deeply, my dear ones, and be courageous with your explorations that they may bring you into the fragrance and flavour of your truth.

This may take some time, but I will be waiting to reveal the next Secreta when you are ready.

That is all I ask, that you be ready.

So my beloved friends, enjoy this beautiful Secreta—it is yours for the asking: "You can make life sweet and fragrant by your thoughts and actions".

Be ever mindful of how you are tending your Soul Garden and the quality of your seeds!

Your ever patient friend of the fragrant world,

Demeter

The Fifth Secreta : Silence and Stillness

Dear friends, I am wondering if the time is right to speak to you of Silence.

If you are to explore this secret, then you will need to have time and space without any distractions.

Do you think that you are ready yet for this?

Silence is a space of great power and also Great Mystery, for when you enter the emptiness that is Silence, you begin to hear the Song of your Soul.

Is this what you are seeking?

I do not want to "put you off" this process of discovery, this inner voyage.

I do not want to frighten you away with something that you cannot yet grasp, so are you ready for Silence?

This is the fifth Secreta: "In Silence you are able to open the door to your self-knowledge. This is like a "short cut" to your Inner Wisdom."

This may seem against my earlier wish that you should not rush, that there is always time, but in the journey to the Great Mystery, the mastery of the Self is the first step or "goal," if you like.

I want you to know success early so that you continue to master the Secretas.

This is my avowed intention in speaking to you today.

In farming the land, you have to know the type of soil with which you are working. This naturally helps you to plant the best crops and create the optimum conditions for growth. This requires careful concentration.

So too it is with your Soul. To grow yourself, you have to know the essential quality of your Soul.

You have to concentrate on the language of your Soul so that you can best know how to grow your tree of life.

We talked of fragrance and flavour, and I hope that these two elements are enriching your life each day, but what about the music of your life?

What does your life sound like?

You can listen in Silence and know if there is harmony or discord.

You can hear if the tune is light and joyous or heavy and dramatic.

So too you can know the music that you need to listen to, the music you wish to hear, and the music which you can compose in your Soul Tuning.

I hope that this is comfortable for you.

I know that your world can be a very noisy, very busy place and that sometimes it is hard to find a place of Silence.

Seek to refresh yourself in the Song of Nature whenever you can, for there is a melody which will nourish your Soul, if you take the time to listen.

Make a space to explore tranquillity when you have time to be, that is when you have time that you are not always "doing.'

It may be once a day, once a week, or once a year.

All you need is to give yourself the chance for peace.

When you meet yourself in this place of peace, you will smile with recognition at the beauty that can exist, that *does* exist, beyond the noise of everyday life.

You will see the beauty of yourself as a reflection of All That Is.

Take your time to listen to your Sacred Song of Life.

You see, the Great Mystery is the source of all things and would communicate with us not in words but in vibrations that resonate.

In the depth of Silence, you can catch this resonance like the bar of a Sacred melody.

In Silence, you can sense and feel more acutely.

Before there was chatter and gossip, there was language; before there was language, there were sound and gesture; before there were sound and gesture, there was Silent knowing.

When you are Silent, you are tapping into this ancient code of knowing, which needs not words.

This is a deeper communication, a fuller resonance than the distortions of word language.

Being Silent is a part of Sacred life

It is a state of connecting with All That Is.

You know this is very simple, but I suspect that you will find it hard.

Now I will shut up and let you practise.

Shhhhhh. You know who!

THE SIXTH SECRETA : BEING ALONE

Well, my friends, have you been enjoying some silence?

I hope that you have found a way to make this a regular part of your lives, for it will help you to survive with sanity where all else may seem crazy!

Today I want to continue on your journey with the Secreta of "Being Alone".

For many people, this is fearsome, and I want to dispel that fear.

Are you ready to look at this, my friends?

I wish that all people had the courage to spend more time alone, for in your world aloneness is associated with loneliness.

This is not what I am talking about, so are we ready to listen and see if there is something which we can learn in our aloneness?

It seems a perpetual occupation to be forever with other people, not just for company or conversation but for constant distraction.

Now I am not suggesting that you should all become hermits.

Far from it, for if you take yourself away from the world then how will you connect with your Humanity?

After all, that is why you are on the Earth at this precise moment in time, because you have chosen the Human experience right at this difficult time.

So do you think that you are ready for this Secreta on aloneness?

This Secreta is: "You are never alone."

Let me explain.

When you are surrounded by other humans you have to listen to their chatter, feel their different vibrations, and react to their neediness. This is a wonderful distraction from Yourself, and it becomes impossible to separate out that which is "You" and that which is "They".

This is interaction, and of course it has a place of great value, but it is not All There Is.

That box with moving pictures is your other companion, so when are you ever alone apart from in your sleep? No wonder some of you have amazing dreams!

When do you have time to get back to being on your own with no distractions, "in your own space", as you say?

When you leave behind all external distractions and let yourself be purely natural, then you begin to learn about that which really matters to you, those behaviours which are genuine.

Not that which you do to attract or influence other people.

Not that which you engage in because you are afraid of your weakness, your vulnerability, or your inner neediness.

At this point of total self-honesty, you are open to the workings of the Great Mystery and you can embrace that which is your heart's true desire, not that which you think you *should* want but that which is true to You.

In this place of Self-Truth, you are also able to connect with your many friends who are in Spirit. This is why you are never alone, but you have to be "alone" to know this.

This is the way to catch your fears and let them blow away with the wind because you no longer need them to restrict you. You can be honest with yourself, and this will help you be stronger and more direct in your dealings with others.

At all costs, you must find this space of truth within yourself or else your life is but a lie, an act of self-deceit which will not bear the fruit to which you have been given the seeds.

If you pretend that you are someone different from whom you are, then you are actively rejecting that which is your "Self".

This kind of rejection leads to imbalance, illness, and unhappiness, so embrace who you are right now, and love your "Self" to bits!

You won't always be the same because you are growing, right?

But now at least you stand a chance of flourishing because you are accepting your birthright, your rootstock if you like.

This is the harvest of the Sixth Secreta.

May it be rich and bountiful as you relinquish dependency on others, so you will begin to recognise the fruit of your own strength and beauty.

It has a fragrance of authenticity. It has the flavour of integrity

Take this aloneness as a precious time, and you will return refreshed and ready to engage with All That Is.

This friend is ever with you, should you seek her,

Demeter

THE THIRD TRIAD

THE SEVENTH SECRETA : THE POWER TO CREATE AND DESTROY

Good evening, my beloved friends.

I am very conscious of the fact that for some of you this may not be a "good" feeling that you have about today, or many other days even.

All around, I see "bad" things happening, people suffering, men and women in pain, anger, desperation, and hunger.

I see many who are lost and unhappy. For this reason, I want you to keep on reading, to persevere with your own journey of understanding, your own path to Peace.

We know that you alone cannot stop the wars, cannot heal the sick, cannot take away the hunger, but if just one of you learns to create goodness in your own lives, then I have been successful in sharing with you each day, each week that you have kept coming back to dig deeper, to discover more.

For each individual who reclaims this Power of "Creation," there is a much wider benefit to humanity than you can see in your immediate field of vision.

So, my friends, the Seventh powerful Secreta is this: "You have the Power to Create, and you have the Power to Destroy."

It is how you choose to use this Power which will then attract creation or destruction into your Life.

This is the Power which each and every one of us holds but has been denied to you for thousands of years, for there are those who would seek to control you for their own power.

Their interest has been in suppression, in delusion, in fear, in intimidation, and in false beliefs.

I don't want you to be deluded, I don't want you to live in fear, I don't want you to live in oppression, I don't want you to live behind false beliefs, and so, my friends, I come to help you realise the nature of your own Power.

I'm not sure if you felt you were ready for this, but I have no time to waste so we must continue to look deeper and deeper at why you are living your fragmented lives, your lives of dissatisfaction, your lives of desire, without ever finding that for which you are searching.

Well, now that you know that **you** can Create and Destroy, you can no longer be looking to blame other people for what is wrong in your life.

To work with this Power, you will have to do some "deep-sea diving" to examine your own depths, your own beliefs about what is in your life and why.

You may well dredge up some mighty rubbish, but deep down you will also find some buried treasure.

It is all a part of who you are, and it is what you choose to do with the rubbish and the treasure that will create the next stage of your journey.

Remember you always have choice so that you can choose to drag the rubbish with you, or you can choose to let it go. You can destroy it.

You can choose to hide the treasure in fear that others might envy it, or you can take it out and give it a polish till it gleams and carry it as a reminder that you like treasure and would like to create some more.

What do you think? Will you even make a choice, or will you be content to just stay exactly where you are for a while and change nothing?

It is always a choice to be still, to lie fallow for a while, but be prepared to move into action later, or all will stagnate within and your chance for certain choices will be lost.

The World cannot be still. It is constantly renewing through Creation and Destruction.

This is the life force you have chosen to access, and you need to know how it works if you are to succeed. This is the Power you can harness when you understand the Secretas of the Great Mystery.

The Great Mystery has endless choices on offer and honours your right to choose for yourselves.

This Seventh Secreta is also about recognising that each choice has a consequence.

When we begin to see this, then we can begin to connect with the Power of Choice. This is where Personal Responsibility is born. Where we make choices out of true preference rather than from imposed expectations, out of mature understanding rather than from distorted beliefs, out of deep Vision rather than from external obligations or the desire for approval and shallow gratification.

The tyrannies of law enforcement and violent power regimes would be reduced to non-events if each individual had the Vision to fully see the consequences of their own actions, for truly the law of returns operates with precision.

As you sow so you shall grow.

Is this sinking into your thinking?

Are you ready to accept responsibility for *all* your thoughts and actions? These are the tools of your Power, be it to Create or Destroy.

I am sure this has given you food for thought.

There will be much work so choose to do it with a passion. We will be returning for the next Secreta when you are ready to step forward in the light of this Power to Create and Destroy.

Such is the way of nature, gentle and nurturing, dramatic and dynamic.

See yourself as this.

Know yourself as part of the same Mystery.

Courage be with you,

D

THE EIGHTH SECRETA : VISION DREAMING

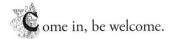ome in, be welcome.

Is this a better day for you today?

No doubt you have been doing some clearing out, both physically and mentally, emotionally and spiritually, eh?

This is the way forward to a clearer sense of being, for how can you begin to Vision your power if you are living in a fog?

Well, my dears, as you will be discovering for yourselves these days, all is not what it seems or even what you were led to believe.

That box in which you have been fitting yourself is far too small for your Dreams and the wonder of your life as you wish to create it now.

It is quite amazing to watch you grow, to watch as you allow yourself to expand in all you do, for life does not have to be lived in a small space if you do not wish it.

Hmmm, this is very powerful thinking now, isn't it?

The Eighth Secreta is about making Dreams come true.

I am sure that this is something you are all ready to listen to so we will go straight ahead, "jumping in the deep end" as you say, isn't it?

What is a Dream?

Not a sleeping dream but a Vision Dream?

Those dreams you have when you let yourself drift away and escape from your routine daily life. This is nothing more than you breathing outside the narrow confines that you have created for your life at this point in time. When you release your physical boundaries, your parameters of

logic, and allow yourself the luxury of imaging a different way of being, these are the Dreams of which I speak today.

Without these, life is very dull indeed, for these Vision Dreams are signposts to your inner desires, your secret wishes, your truest passions. If we suppress them, we will never know the choices we have missed, for these point the way to possibilities that are open to us.

They are your "seedbed" of choices.

So first of all, allow yourself a rich life of Vision Dreaming.

Some of you will have already opened this door by fulfilling the learning in the earlier secrets, but for those of you who are holding back (in fear?), be not afraid to let reality slide and experience this other way of "seeing". (Go back if you need to Silence, Aloneness, Fragrance and Flavour, and your tree of life.)

This is the first step, for how can Dreams come true if you are never letting them have a home in your way of being?

This is the easy part and the fun part, for next you have to begin to believe that the Dream which you have chosen, will become reality for you. This belief is very hard because it runs against the body of teaching, which would have you believe that life is meant to be hard and that you do not deserve to have "Riches in Life".

The Great Mystery would want you to reap what you sow, not to be stingy and fearful in the sowing so that you reap a meagre harvest.

When you can accept this, then you will begin to pay attention to that which you are sowing and you will take great care to nurture your "crops," for you will want to harvest the best rewards. And so you shall.

Riches in life are not only for the privileged few.

The Great Mystery would want all to share in the richness in life, for all to realise their Dreams and keep creating fulfilment. From fulfilment comes generosity, enthusiasm, inspiration and motivation.

While the thinking in your world is dedicated to making people conform, to fit into a space that is too small, which gives no room for growth, for personal genius to emerge, so there will be a dramatic downward spiral in fulfilment, motivation, and inspiration.

This you see as an increase in depression, deviancy, and suicide.

These are Broken Dream syndromes, and there is no way they are the reflection of Personal Power. These are crushed souls who have ceased to find a way to breathe life into their Dreams.

Now do you see why this "conspiracy" of Global Power and repression has to be stopped?

Why I must speak loudly and clearly even though your "liberal" society will not welcome all I have to say?

So be it.

There is a time, and it is now.

I want you to understand with no illusion that there is space for All, and each person must take responsibility for the Self. You are all part of the one Great Mystery, and each one is affected by the parts of the whole.

Your decisions, your choices have an impact for the whole, and it is in this perspective that you begin to make your own Dreams come true.

When you finally succeed, it is because you have had the courage to take the steps from your Vision Dream to fulfilment.

There can be no concrete taste of success without you starting to *walk your talk*. Doing and Being must partner each other for the threshold of the Vision time to be crossed over into this concrete dimension.

So you see, this is another two-part secret.

"Your Vision Dreams show the seeds which your Soul would have you plant in your Life Garden.

Your harvest shows the work which you have done to care and nurture for your own fulfilment."

Be sure that you will attract the help and opportunities which you require for your success once you have chosen your dream.

Remember that you are never alone.

Well, our next Secreta will help you along the way with this, but now I feel that it is time to let you digest that which I have shared today, so I will leave you for now, my friends, but come back just as soon as you are ready to accept a little more to help you cultivate your "Soul" harvest.

Till then,

Demeter

The Ninth Secreta : The Balance
of the dark and the Light

Today, my friends, I am preparing the final Secret of the Third Triad, a powerful insight for your further advancement in the story of the Great Mystery.

I welcome you and await your presence, in that state of open being which will allow this Great Secret to pass into your knowingness.

Are you ready, do you think?

Let us go back over your past preparedness to make sure that all is well in your journey so far.

Are you taking more time to enjoy your lives?

Are you sensing more carefully the etheric value of your life in fragrance, flavour, music, and charm?

Are you resting with yourself in a place of peace?

Are you connecting with your sense of beauty?

Are you accepting that you have the power to create change?

Are you witnessing the effect of your power to make your dreams come true?

Then you have worked well, my dear friends, and I would reward you with this Secreta, which I beg you not to share until you know for yourself that it is true.

So, let us be ready, open and listening, ready to vision and sense the truth of what you read.

The Ninth Secreta is based on the balance of dark and light, and we have to take a little journey to gather the full importance of this aspect of the Great Mystery for you see the Great Mystery is the source of both dark and light.

We have witnessed the rejection of the dark side as we have watched the morality of man's belief systems shrink the understanding of the Natural Way of Justice.

There has been a fear of the dark as it has been associated with acts of pain and terror.

It has been labelled "bad" in the context of man's understanding, and it has been set in opposition to the light which has been named "good."

My friends, this is too limiting by far, for there is good and bad in your understanding of the dark and the light.

I want you to think why this has come to be.

I want you to think why all things of the Moon side have been classified as bad and pushed away when this is one full half of the work of the Great Mystery.

Let me talk to you a moment of this Moon side.

As you know, the Moon is controlling the tides and all that is fluid. She is gentle yet full of force, she is soft yet persistent, she flows around great obstacles, and she shifts solid matter in her endless pull.

She is the source of all things feminine and, with her, you will identify with your inner drive to create, your natural tendency to pulse without the need for time, your power to sense beyond reason that which is right for you.

She brings great giftedness to those who relent their need for all things logical.

She is the Mother of our Times, and we owe her our full attention if we are to enter into our wholeness.

Could this rejection be simply the fear of Man to control that which cannot be controlled?

I ask you to think on this for each one of you, male and female, has been closed down by this narrow understanding of the workings of All That Is.

Too easy it has been to dismiss the dark side as evil, as the road to your religious hell, as the way of devil's work and black magic.

This is not the way of the Great Mystery, to cast people away as "sinners."

This is not the true darkness, and it is not for man to sit in judgement of the dark or the light.

The Great Mystery moves through Pure Love and accepts all things as right for that intention.

This I know is a vital challenge to that which pervades your society as morality, that which parades as Justice, but you see the Great Mystery embraces all of time and space and the truth of what is right far exceeds the boundaries of your narrow vision from your Earth view.

The Secreta you see is that "Dark is not Bad".

If you cannot embrace the totality of who you are, then you too are rejecting a part of yourself and a part of the Great Mystery.

When we can accept this, then we come back to the Natural Laws and our decisions are made on the basis of our own guidance and not the fear of that to which we have been told to conform.

The Nazarene, your beloved Jesus, told you simply,

"Do unto others as you would have them do unto you."

That is to accept the Natural Laws and let them guide you not out of fear but out of desire for your own well-being, your own sense of peace, and your own belief in the best, for yourself and therefore for others.

Without darkness there can be no light, so let not your life be so full of pursuit of one at the expense of the other.

To embrace the dark brings you the gifts of forgiveness, humility, surrender and finally wholeness.

I have seen great pride and spiritual arrogance in "followers of the light" for they are intent on their own enlightenment and pursue the "path" with fervour. This can lead to feelings of superiority, and creates the divides between "believers" and "nonbelievers".

We are all one, and any mindset which seeks to create a separation is not the way forward for us at this point in our history.

This is why this message is reaching you today and why you are being encouraged to recognise that which is right and wrong for yourself.

The Great Mystery is working to bring all together in Natural Justice. This is the Justice of the heart, not of man's making.

It requires no punishments, for eventually the repercussions of wrong behaviour (i.e., that which is harmful to others) will be immediate and will bring each one back to the original state of caring that the Great Mystery desires.

This cannot happen until each individual reaches wholeness (healedness).

Have you seen how many "healers" there are in your part of the world? This is part of the Great Preparation for Wholeness.

This is the healing of the separation.

This is the healing of the Dark and the Light.

This is the healing of the divisions of All That Is.

You are a part of this, and the Great Mystery is indeed joyous at the number of her people who are finding their way back to the Source.

Keep embracing all that you are, and you will reach the end of your journey with honours.

So be it, my friends, for I am guiding you each step of the way.

I am Demeter,

Goddess of the Dark and the Light,

Goddess of the Fallow and the Full,

Goddess who is seeking to enter your hearts and heal the World.

Be Beloved of Your whole selves,

Demeter

THE FOURTH TRIAD

THE TENTH SECRETA : THE GREAT LOVE

Be at peace with who you are, and be at peace with what is happening in your lives.

I ask today how you are faring with this your increase in knowingness.

I wish you many fulfilments, for this is the way of *great progress* in the *Mysteries of Life.*

Who do you think **you** are now?

Is this a different you from the one who started reading at the first page of these Secretas, or is it the same person with expanded vision sight and wisdom?

What do you think?

How do you feel?

I am always asking you these things for no matter how much I am telling you, it is of no value to you, or anyone else, if first you are not feeling it the whole way through your being.

To feel it is to fully recognise the changes which you are witnessing in yourself and how you are living your life.

Is life any easier for you now?

Is life any simpler?

Is life any more enjoyable?

Is what you are creating that of which you dream, or are there still the remnants of instilled fear which are stopping you?

Are you accepting that which *is* more readily, as that which has to be for this space in your time, for that which has been created so far?

And are you ready to travel farther, my friends, for your journey is almost complete?

The Secretas, they are thirteen, and here we are at the Tenth Secreta already.

I am witnessing many changes in many small but significant ways.

This is the way of Natural Change, where the many influence the few, rather than the few who control the many.

Never doubt that you and you and you can together create a better world, and the basis of this needs to be your wholeness.

Now the next Triad deals of course with the most important issue of your "healedness", and that is the nature of Love, for Love is the tool that heals all woundedness and cures all the hurts of the heart.

You may have found that stepping into the dark with the Ninth Secreta was the most fearsome part of your journey so far, but this had to be so for you to reclaim all that is You.

I trust you are comfortable now with who You are.

The Tenth Secreta is this: "You are to love yourself however wounded you are, and this will heal your very essence. This will replenish your "soul soil" so that once more you can begin to grow and harvest that which is your heart's desiring."

Love brings ease when you are fallow, energy when you are in growth, strength for harvest when it is time to reap, and the joy of fullness in your rewards when it is time to sit and savour the fruits of your labours.

Love is the nutrition for enriching your Soul Crop, and it is up to you how you cultivate it and apply it.

The Love which is the Great Mystery is no longer a secret and no longer needs to hide or be concealed by those who would fear its power.

It is for each and every one of you to discover in your own way and your own good time . . . when you are ready.

There is no other Power which can transform the destiny of your life.

Is this what you want?

Love is the Life Force which drives all things of the Natural World, but humans have taken a convoluted journey to reach this destination of knowingness, acceptance, and peace of being.

Now you are already wise and will know that the love which creates the sexual attraction of relationships is but a minor strand of the richness of Great Love, which is the Original Source of Joy and Healing on this Earth Plane.

The Love of desire and romance is a beautiful thing that causes people to flourish, to try to give of their best and to be caring and protective of another.

That which is Mother Love is also a magnificent thing which causes men and women to yearn for the best for their children, to try to be protective, to wish to provide and support another fragile being, to take responsibility for that which they have created.

The Great Love of which I now speak is a passion that feeds the Soul and inspires each one to connect with the Love aspect of themselves, that is a mirror of the greatest beauty in the World.

You cannot love without feeling this beauty.

The Great Love opens up your heart, expands your generosity, fuels your desire to grow and change, creates great compassion, reduces fears and gives you courage to challenge yourself and overcome the pain of the World.

So, where is this Great Love in your life?

Has it got a space?

Is it large or small?

Is it central or in a box at the side?

What space do you give to Love?

Many people are feeling that love is something which they can open and close like a purse of coins, that it is a currency to be controlling of.

Rubbish!

The more Love you give, the more you will generate and the more you will receive, for this more accurately than any other evidence is the "Natural Law of Returns" in action.

Love needs to be given freedom to multiply, to expand, to travel, and share. It needs not a tight and fearsome space.

Of its own power, Love will return and multiply when it is given freely, that is with no conditions, no neediness in the offering, and no contract of "part exchange" in small print.

For Love brings freedom, freedom for you to be who you are and freedom for each and every one of you to lift your "beingness" into giftedness.

Be at peace with who You are, but give yourself permission to spread your wings and feel the Joy of flight.

This is where you fly at one with the Great Mystery and let Love steer your course through the stars by the compass of your heart.

How will you ever know the truth of this secret if you do not surrender to the Power of Love and open your heart to the way of fearlessness?

I bid you find this way which has been ever open to you, my friends of beauty and delight.

Share and enjoy, for this is the Tenth Secreta.

Yours in loving kindness,

Demeter

THE ELEVENTH SECRETA : INSPIRATION, VISION, HOPE

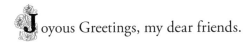oyous Greetings, my dear friends.

I wish you all the joy of your labours so far.

Truly, we are coming to the richness of your harvest, for you have laboured long and hard, so the rewards will be of the most beneficial kind for yourself and also for those around you . . . for who does not enjoy to see a flower in full bloom?

Who does not enjoy to share the luscious ripeness of a fruit in full juice?

Who does not enjoy the beauty of a feast?

For feast is what you will have to share when you are working with the Natural Laws of growth and season, of the time for ebb and flow.

So this is your learning of the Secretas in action.

Like anything else, the more that you are practising, the more you will becoming skilled until you are a "Master" yourself.

Do not give up if all has not eventuated as you planned, rather be grateful that you learnt to hope and try again, until you truly master that which is difficult for you.

These Secretas are not negotiable.

That is for each of you. There is a pathway waiting to ease the flow of your life, once you learn the secrets of working in the Natural Way, once you can accept this position of responsibility for Your Self, Your actions, Your feelings, Your decisions.

This is how you progress with ease.

With Love in your heart, anything is possible, so today we want to look at how you are using this wondrous "ingredient".

If you have been practising the essence of the Tenth Secreta, then you will already be finding that your life is richer, that the quality is finer, that the memories are sweeter.

Is this so?

I would ask you to repeat this "heart work" if you are in doubt.

Remember that regardless of who, or what, you are, you cannot reach Your fullness, Your harvest, until you are loving every part of Yourself.

Let us take this a little further for this Eleventh Secreta requires us to discover the expansiveness of our love, and this cannot be a finding until you have embraced your wholeness.

The Great Love has no equal.

This means it cannot be manufactured, it cannot be faked, and it cannot be substituted with "lesser value" feelings. It cannot be bought.

This Great Love of which we speak is pure and brilliant. It has a resonance which creates a shimmer around you.

It never wavers, not even when the day is cloudy. It is still a shining light.

This is what our Eleventh Secreta tells us: "This Great Love is what creates sparks of Inspiration, of Vision, of Hope. It is the signature of the Great Mystery."

Wherever you see, hear, touch, or create Great works of Art, then know that the Great Mystery has been at work.

Know also that where you see or practise Great Compassion, therein you will be touched by the work of the Great Mystery.

Where you witness the depths of despair, there also are the glimmers of hope which the Great Mystery uses to penetrate the all-engulfing pain and sorrow.

Wherever humankind is seeking to achieve progress for the greater good, so too you will see the evidence of the Great Mystery at work with this tool, which is called Love.

It is as boundless as the ocean, it is more solid than the mountain rocks, and it is beyond the brightest star.

Dear ones, I wish that you begin to understand that Great Love cannot always fill your hearts, and for this you must not despair.

It is part of the Human condition to weave in and out of the light and the dark, but, just as I have asked you to discover that which is your darkest place, so I would desire that you also allow your selves to embrace that which gives you brilliance.

For some this is a very uncomfortable space, for once again much has been taught to prevent you from knowing of the power of This Great Love, which is but a part of your birthright.

The Great Mystery would have you share this dimension of your beingness so that all others can be inspired by your efforts.

You will all have experienced flashes of this dazzling union when inspiration strikes, when vision is clear, when hope springs from the dark.

You will be knowing that of which I speak, but now it is your task to deliver this part of yourself for the Harvest.

There are no guidelines, for when you are reaching this level of your knowingness you are receiving your own guidance, and if you have prepared your Soul soil well, then you are ready to follow the "messages" which are planted as seeds in your heart.

You see, we are nearing the fullness of your year and having nurtured your Soul garden with tenderness this year, so you will be able to trust yourself with the tender care of next year's "crop."

These Secretas stand the test of all time and will ensure that you continue to succeed.

I am honoured to have been able to bear the Mystery to you through this channel.

Before we meet again, I want you to practise the following.

Be Love.

Be Love for all around to be enlightened by your shining.

Be Love because it is the dazzle of the Great Mystery, which is Secret no more.

Be Welcome and take your place before we are completing the Fourth Triad.

This will be the completion of The Golden Triangle.

Be blessed as Shining Ones,

Yours in Great Beauty,

Demeter

THE TWELFTH SECRETA : TRUTH

Greetings, dear ones of the heart.

It is with great joy that I am here to share with you this final Secreta of the Triad of the Heart, that which is golden and shining in your lives.

So, we reach our zenith, and you can walk away forever in your own Sacredness.

If by now you are wondering what all the fuss is about, what it is that you have been searching for, striving for, struggling with, then you will be able to sit back with a quiet smile, for all that you have learnt on this your Sacred journey has been simply that of which you already knew but dared not believe!

My beautiful friends, this is Your Story, this is Your Sacredness, and this is Your Power.

It is not me or any other "leader" whom you may have been following. Quite simply, it is Yourself.

So, are we ready to reveal this last and final layer of Your protectedness?

Are we ready to see the Truth of who we are?

Are we ready for life to be much easier?

Well, so be it, my friends, for this final secret of our Golden Triad is this: "The Truth is simple, and it resides within the heart of each and every one of you."

How simple is that, my friends?

All your looking for special ways, for secret doings, for the answer outside, and all the time you need go no farther than your own self.

This Truth of which I speak is the truth of who you are as a part of the Great Mystery.

When you are accepting of this, my beloved ones, then you can truly relax and learn to trust, for what is it that you have troubles with in your own life but your fear of your own limitations, your lack of trust in Yourself?

This is not the place where faith resides, and I would have you know the faith you need is not in me or any other deity, but it is in nothing more than Your Own Self, Your Own power to create, Your Own responsibility for Your Life.

Now this is an awesome Truth for some of you, and yet you have been travelling towards it for sometime so do not be afraid now to take this final step and embrace that which is clear and simple.

As you recognise yourself as a part of the Whole from which we all transcend, then you will be accepting of All That Is.

You will know that for each separate being, there is a Personal Truth which each has created, as well as the bigger Truth of which we have spoken, which is the Natural Law of Returns.

This abiding Truth is the source of Your power, and you can use it to attract that which you desire, for now you will understand the consequential truth of your every action.

You will stand tall and aim straight.

You will nurture those who are struggling beside you.

You will show others the Truth of who you are by the way in which you live your life.

This is the full measure of Your Truth.

Ask yourself these questions: How are you using the gifts you have been given? How are you spending your time and your money? How are you feeling when there is suffering amongst you? How are you celebrating your harvest? How are you sharing with others? Is your life a sacred path? Where is your faith? Is there love in your heart? Is there acceptance of your humanity?

These are indicators of where your life is rooted, of the seeds you have sown, of the commitment you have given to growing and nurturing Yourself.

Seek the answers in your own Soul space, and be sure that you are not rejecting or hiding one little bit of who you are.

Only when this embracement of Your whole self is complete will you be ready to accept this simple Secreta of the Truth.

So my dearest gardeners of the Soul, is this giving you the answers for yourself?

I hope so, for then you are working to improve the harvest for yourself and all those around you, seen and unseen, for you know that we are truly rejoicing when we see you coming home to Yourself in Beauty.

Walk with Truth, my friends, and you will soon be dancing with your Joy.

In celebration, I am your bounteous partner.

Deo

ZENITH

THE THIRTEENTH SECRETA : CELEBRATING HARVEST

For this our final gathering, I ask that bring your open hearts.

All that we have discovered, my fellow gardeners, is of no use if there is a tightness and resistance in the heart.

Do you have this open heart, my friends?

Are you prepared for your freedom in the outside world with no one to account to but your own true self?

This is the finale, before your onward journey.

If you step forward and offer yourself for the Sacred Journey, then be sure you are totally accepting of all that you have learnt so far, for there can be no going back once you have taken this final learnedness into your heart.

Be sure the Natural Law of Returns is swift and accurate, for there is no one to blame now but yourself if you do not like the consequences.

Think well, my Soul Initiates.

Sit awhile before you decide.

No need for rushing; remember our first Secreta?

Feel the fragrance of where you are now, and listen to the music of your life as you are creating it.

Do you like it?

 Tricia mary Lee

Remember there is always choice and you can choose, even now, to stay exactly where you are until you are ready.

Is this comfortable for you?

Please, and I do plead with you, be gentle with yourself, be forgiving of yourself where you have not quite understood with the heart. Be courageous in your efforts to do your best, and be remembering at all times that you will see come into bloom that which you have sown—only if you continue to nurture and create conditions for growth.

I beg you at this stage to draw very close to the ways of nature and observe the way that prize gardeners tend their seedlings. You are like saplings at this stage and truly I would have you grow to full strength and maturity so that you will bear the ripest fruits. This is the heart's desire of all Mothers.

I am reluctant to release you before you have the strength to survive, for truly there is much wilderness in your world, and I pray that I have done my job well in tending you as "Soul Gardeners".

So, my tender friends, please receive this, my final gift to you, as a token of my gratitude for your attendance here at these little "passionellas" and I commend each and every one of you who has chosen to travel with me on this Sacred Pathway.

Our Zenith has to be that which will sustain you in all weathers, for you will need much sustenance to fill your garden amidst the chaos of the World as we see it at the moment.

This is it: "Be ever open, for then you will receive the richness of that which you are deserving."

You see, my friends, so many people plant seeds and then neglect them, forget about them, change their minds about them, wish for more or different, or reject with scorn all that they have grown and achieved.

This is not the way of Soul Gardening.

The heart is the place of exchange, of photosynthesis if you like, only your energy source is Great Love.

This is the currency of the heart and, if the heart is open, then the vibrations of Love can sustain the body even in the hardest times. But if the heart is closed, then the energy which would sustain you is unable to enter and life begins to shrink and shrivel as a plant without water and sunlight.

You are no different to all that grows, my beloved ones, but your energy needs to be sustained by Love.

Your steps to Sacredness help to create a Sacred Space where it feels safe to open your heart. All of your steps so far will be fruitless if you are not prepared to allow your heart to be vulnerable. It is the only way that you can access the source of Love, and once you are trusting of this, then you will feel safe to let your heart be ever open.

There needs to be no fear of pain now, for what is pain but that which we are creating to help us change the way we are living? So let yourself feel the pain, and do not be closing the heart and hiding from it.

Consider it a messenger who will help you if you do but listen. So much, my friends, I would want to protect you, but this is not the way for you to grow in true strength.

Therefore, I must leave you with these "tools" which have been preserved for so long but which now must return to full and active use for the richness of your lives to be realised and the advancement of the whole human race to take place.

No more hiding, no more Secretas, no more wishing away that which you have created.

Stand up and Be with Yourself in what You have created.

Go, my treasured ones. Be Sacred in all you do, and be in the heart-full place for your truth to shine as an example for those around you.

You are commended as Keepers of the Great Soul Garden.

May it forever inspire you to Greatness.

I abide with you all,

Demeter

EPILOGUE

A PARTING GIFT

As the full year cycle is now complete, we must prepare for your release in order that you can find your own way on that which is your chosen path.

As your friend, I have shared the fruits of my wisdom, and you now likewise must seek to seed and bear "fruit" which you can share. In being Soul Gardeners, you will attract attention and you will yourselves stand as examples of the best that the Great Mystery can harvest . . . the "Cream of the Crop".

When you are ready, you can share that which you have learnt on this, your journey to the Great Mystery, as this is another way of sowing seeds, of creating new growth and thereby a bigger harvest for the World.

Be clear, my divine dwellers on Earth.

Be clear what your intention is.

Be clear on that which you desire.

You do not need me to give you the details of how to proceed each and every time. Have faith in your own process that you may sense when to adjust your "sowing" and "reaping", that you may know the best way to create that which you are choosing. "Trust yourself to know yourself" (Oracle at Delphi).

Be your own guide in the light of Your own wisdom.

Be clear in your patterns of thought, and your intentions will hold fast. Be clear in your actions. Be remembering to consider all the consequences as you are able to Vision them from your place of standing.

Finally, as a Mother I wish for you the following:

I wish for you to choose that which you most desire and for there to be happiness within.

I wish for you to enjoy the fruits of your harvest before you choose to sow again.

I wish for there to be no rushing but that you must choose your own pace, your own pathway. This is the place of your Power.

I wish for you to accept all the fruits of your harvest, even if to you they seem imperfect. That which is imperfect has much to teach us, so embrace it readily and be comforted in your own imperfections.

Beloved ones, I am bound to offer these, the fruits of my harvest, for you to "taste," to choose for yourself. There is no "must" or "ought", just offerings for your Earth Journey.

I give Great Thanks for Your time, for Your efforts, for Your determination to create a better World.

You will create your own rewards in this way.

I bid you well on your journey.

Be clear, and choose wisely.

That is all I can offer.

Beloved Goddess of the Fruits,

Demeter Theomophoria

The Demeter Story

DEMETER: GODDESS OF THE ANCIENT WORLD

In the Ancient world, before the birth of Christ, the civilisations of Greece and Rome placed their spiritual beliefs and destiny in a number of Gods and Goddesses often referred to as the Pantheon.

Demeter is acknowledged as one of the original twelve deities at the Athenaeum in Greece. In Roman culture, her name was changed to Ceres.

Demeter was worshipped as the Goddess of the Earth from the time of the Bronze Age, for it was believed that she bestowed the gift of cultivation on the Ancient peoples, thus giving them the gift of civilisation and settlement by releasing them from a nomadic lifestyle.

Once people could cultivate their food and grow crops, they were no longer totally dependent on hunting and animals for their sustenance.

This marked a significant leap forward in man's relationship with the natural world and thereby with his sense of Earth-linked spirituality.

There are many legends surrounding these ancient times and the Gods and Goddesses who were worshipped and revered by the peoples of that time. The most famous legend that gives us insight into Demeter, the Goddess and Earth Mother figure, is in her role as mother to Persephone, whose father was the great God Zeus.

It is believed that Demeter lived on the island of Crete. Her daughter, Persephone, was captured as a beautiful young woman, raped, and taken to Hades in the Underworld by the God Pluto.

Demeter was absolutely distraught and went searching for her daughter from the island of Crete to the mainland of Greece.

In her grief, she refused to let any new seeds sprout from the Earth until her daughter was returned to her. Finally, Zeus was able to find and command the return of Persephone, for which, as a thanksgiving, Demeter granted the gift of cultivation and the art of agriculture.

However, there was a "deal" to Persephone's return, and that was she had to return to the Underworld for a third of the year, thereby allowing her to spend two-thirds of the year with her beloved mother.

While she was away, the land lay fallow, but when she returned the fields burst into flower and the trees began to shoot leaves and later bear fruits.

This gives us an idea of how Demeter suffered the heartache of motherhood, how she experienced every mother's worst fear of losing her precious child, and how she then can understand our love for our children and our grief if they are harmed in any way. Her commitment to family as the basis of society and our world is of paramount importance, as we can see from her teachings.

The poppy flower and the fig are popular symbols that have been associated with Demeter through the ages. (And as I write this, in true symbolic synchronicity, there is, just a little further along my road, a glorious, mature fig tree heavily laden with fruit which is free to passers-by!)

Bees also are symbolic of her presence as they were considered her servants, being the pollinators of all fruits and flowers, making honey a sacred food from the Goddess.

In Greece, at Mycalessus, there was a sanctuary devoted to Demeter, where it was said that the fruits and flowers placed at the foot of her statue preserved their freshness far beyond the usual timeline.

Elsewhere there was Demeter's Wood, an abundant forest, which contained pine and elm trees as well as wild apples and pears.

Each year in Ancient Greece, in September, there was a celebration called The Festival of Theomophoria. This was for married women only and honoured their legitimate status as wives. By entering a conjugal union of marriage, the young women were seen to have escaped the risk of promiscuous relationships and the waste of their "seeds". Marriage was seen as a denunciation of savagery, as a civilised option to the old sport of "virgin hunting" and rape.

This celebration lasted for six days and coincided with the ritual of sowing seeds for crops in the northern hemisphere season of autumn. The final day of this festival was called "Beautiful Birth".

We can see here how Demeter was revered as a powerful advocate of "sacred union" and the creation of a civilised approach to sexuality and the relationship of marriage. This clearly marked a move away from previous practices towards women, where their honour and sexuality were not respected or highly valued.

She truly stands as an ancient forerunner for women's rights.

There is one story in the ancient legends in which we are told that the God Adonis, contrary to the teachings of Demeter, encouraged his followers to grow gardens in only eight days by using shallow stone pots. The results were crops without fruits; the plants were immature and without proper root systems because they had not been nourished or allowed to develop over the fullness of time. (This can be seen as a direct reflection of her teachings on *Time* in the manuscript.)

Demeter tells us in the Third Secreta of her manuscript, "No matter how fancy you make it look, it will not bear fruit so be sure to nourish your Soul". (Remembering the soul is as the Earth's soil). This seems to be a direct reference to the shallow work of Adonis.

These legends in history give us insight and understanding into the nature of Demeter, helping us realise why and how she would want to help us as women at this time of great challenge and change.

Her gentle, caring energy is every bit that of a Mother whilst her awareness of our spiritual needs is truly that of a Goddess.

Her wisdom translates from the physical to the metaphysical, and we are blessed as we work our Soul soil with all the tools she puts at our disposal.

THE MYSTERIES : FROM ELEUSIS IN ANCIENT GREECE TO HERE AND NOW

The city of Eleusis lies 14 miles to the west of Athens in the Mediterranean country we know as Greece.

In the Ancient World, in the city of Eleusis, there was an annual celebration of 'The Mysteries' in honour of the Great Goddess Demeter who, it was believed, had given mankind the gift of cultivation and agriculture.

"Let us recall that the rites of Eleusis were held for some 2,000 years; that for two thousand years civilized humanity was sustained and ennobled by these rites. Then we shall be able to appreciate the meaning and importance of Eleusis and of the cult of Demeter in the Pre-Christian era." G. E. Mylonas

The legend holds that when Demeter was searching, in her grief, for Persephone her daughter, she was given shelter by the royal family of Eleusis and she subsequently helped to nurse their youngest son, Demophon, who was a sickly babe.

With Demeter's nourishment, Demophon grew strong and so her reputation for raising "good seeds" was enhanced. In return the royal family helped Demeter to find Persephone, and so she gave the rites for the Sacred Mysteries to the Princes of Eleusis. They were her way of thanksgiving for the return of her daughter from Pluto, the God of the Underworld.

There are still remains of her Temple at Eleusis today, but in pre-Christian times the Temple was large and housed a "Hierophant" or High Priest as well as a Sanctuary, which housed several Priestesses, who were allowed no communion with men.

This Temple was the site for the celebration of The Mysteries

The High Priestess of Demeter's Temple lived at the Sacred House and she was responsible for taking the role of Demeter in the pageant of The Mysteries. In addition it is known that there were various other "officiates" who performed different tasks :

- Iachygogos : the Priest who accompanied the procession from Athens to Eleusis for those called 'Initiates'.
- Hydranos : who purified the initiates by sprinkling water over them.
- Neokoras : who was responsible for cleaning the Sanctuary
- Phaethyntes : who cleaned the statue of Demeter, the Divine Goddess

The Priest and Priestesses were central to the annual celebration of The Sacred Mysteries at Eleusis, of which there were three separate parts : The Lesser Mysteries, The Greater Mysteries and The Epopteia.

Before the celebrations could commence, in the sacred month of Boedromion, which is equivalent to September-October in our calendar, there was called a truce for the preceding 55 days so that a special messenger could be sent out to call for the first fruits of the harvest from as far away as Egypt, Syria and Antioch. These states then sent a special delegation to Athens with "tithes" in grateful recognition for the bounteous gifts of the Goddess Demeter.

The Mysteries were then celebrated over a period of ten days in Boedromion.

They started on the 14th day of Boedromion when the "Hiera", the Sacred relics of Demeter, were carried by the Priestesses in procession from the Temple at Eleusis to Athens. Originally of course this would have been on foot, but there is evidence from 408 BC that two chariots were used.

The procession would stop outside Athens at the Sacred Fig Tree where legend holds that Demeter stopped on her journey to Eleusis. Here the people of Athens would meet the procession and then escort it to the Sanctuary at the Acropolis where the Hiera would be safely deposited with the Priestess of Athena.

On the 15th day of Boedromion there was a proclamation calling for all the Initiates who had been undertaking the cleansing rituals of the Lesser Mysteries to formally join the procession for the commencement of the celebration of The Mysteries at Eleusis.

The Lesser Mysteries

The first part of the celebration, which was known as The Lesser Mysteries, was open to the general public, taking place as a gathering on the east bank of the River Illisus. The purpose was

to share in the cleansing rites there, for purifying the body and mind in order to create that state of being which would be receptive and clear for the communication of the Greater Mysteries. This lasted for several days and would have no doubt been a joyous time of symbolic release and shared festivities. The Secretas of the First Triad of Demeter's Manuscript closely parallel this process of cleansing and preparation, as we are guided to begin to look at our lives in greater depth. We are encouraged to start and identify those things that we wish to release, those attitudes we wish to change, those "fruits" we wish to seed and nurture for our further growth and harvest. The whole process of *Soul Gardening* as Demeter describes it, begins first with the preparation of our "soil", our inner landscape.

The element of cleansing is a common feature of all spiritual paths and so is that of immersion in water, which is considered a sacred rite for those entering a deeper commitment to their "faith". By washing away the old, the way is open to be reborn for the new way, that of a conscious relationship with the Divine, the dance with the mystery of life as Sacred.

On the 19th day of Boedromion, after a trip to the sea for further washing and cleansing, there was a feast involving the sacrifice of pigs. Dancing and music would also have played a part in this mass festival in honour of the Great Goddess. Those Initiates who were to proceed to the celebration of the Greater Mysteries then prepared to travel to Eleusis, wearing festive clothing and each crowned with a wreath of myrtle. There were donkeys to carry all the heavy baggage of the procession, which was led proudly by Iacchos, the torch-bearer. The Priests and Priestesses would follow, treading the Sacred pathway back to the Temple at Eleusis, to arrive by torchlight with the Initiates singing and dancing in honour of their beloved Goddess.

The Greater Mysteries

The second part of the celebration of the rites in honour of Demeter, was called The Greater Mysteries, and these commenced at the Temple on the 20th day of Boedromion.

The Initiates, tired from their long night procession would first rest and then enter a period of fasting for complete purification, before the "Night of the Telete", when the Mysteries were revealed. The crowns of myrtle were exchanged for garlands with ribbons before the Initiates entered the "Telesterion", or inner Temple, where the Mysteries took place.

As a part of the inner temple ritual, it is known that there was a re-enactment by the Priests and Priestesses, of the "Dromena", the story of Demeter's search for Persephone and her return from the underworld. There was also a ritual called the "Deikynma" which involved the showing of the Sacred relics.

Building the energy with sound, there was also the "Legomena" part of the ritual, where liturgical verses were sung or chanted led by the Priests and Priestesses.

However, true to the Sacred nature of this very personal night of Divine revelation, celebration and ritual, the actual heart of The Greater Mysteries has never been publicly revealed. To this day, the secrets have been kept and honoured, as all the Initiates were sworn to secrecy, bound not to reveal their personal experiences. There has been endless research and conjecture but still The Mysteries have remained elusive, shrouded in the cloak of what is Sacred, held behind the veil that separates this world from the next. We can however clearly see the way that the new religion of the Christian church, simply continued with many of the old traditions of the Sacred way, but under a different name.

Sophocles wrote, "Thrice happy are those mortals who having seen the rites, depart for Hades; for to them alone is it granted to have true life there; to the rest all is evil."

In the Hymn to Demeter, Homer tells us, "Happy is he among men upon earth who has seen these Mysteries."

In bringing forward this Manuscript, I believe Demeter, is breaking her seal of silence, of secrecy, as she acts for the Great Mystery to bring us back into close and sacred union with life and *All that Is*. She is determined that we will know of our right to have a personal and intimate relationship with the Great Mystery and that we also should accept the power and responsibility that comes with this knowledge.

"Whatever the substance and meaning of the Mysteries was, the fact remains that the cult of Eleusis satisfied the most sincere longings and the deepest yearnings of the human heart. The Initiates returned from their pilgrimage to Eleusis full of joy and happiness, with the fear of death diminished and the strengthened hope of a better life in the world of the shadows." G E Mylonas

The Initiates completed their night in the Temple and on the 22nd day of Boedromion there was another special celebration, this time held in honour of the Rites of the Dead, again with much singing and dancing.

This part of the Mysteries has a distinct parallel to our Third Triad, where we are led to look at the "dark side" or the hidden aspects of ourselves, and embrace the wonderful totality of our beings, before we depart this earthly life.

I find a wonderful, reassuring synchronicity, in that of all the twists and turns of my own life since 2000, I have eventually been led to tackle what is regarded in our society as the 'last taboo', becoming not only a Celebrant for funerals, weddings namings and other life rites and blessings, but also presenting workshops on "Sacred Soul Transition" for those who are ready to talk about how we can embrace the fullness and beauty at the ending of life's journey. Shifting the way we think and feel about death, or "departure", and releasing the fear of "heaven or hell", seems a vital step in moving on from the strict western religious grip on the business of death, to a more personal relationship with the Divine and a responsibility for how we live, love and therefore finally die.

Demeter herself seems to want us to engage with the whole cycle of life in a fearless way and we cannot do this without first confronting, understanding and releasing our pain, our suffering, our "woundedness". As a mother who herself suffered the torment of a lost child, she understands only too well the lessons of these feelings and the costs of burying them rather than expressing them fearlessly.

The symbolic loss of innocence and the gaining of wisdom through experience, ie : the journey to the underworld, through the "dark night of the soul", is a myth which has been repeated throughout human history. This would seem to be the vital lesson that is essential in the journey to be human, to be incarnate, and learn the great lessons of "embodiment".

"The confidence developed in the hearts of the heroes initiated in the Mysteries was not due to their preview of the horrors of the lower world, but to their belief that Initiation provided them with a band of communion and friendship with the august divinities in control of that world." G E Mylonas.

The Epopteia

Finally, for a very select few of the Initiates, The Epopteia was the third part of The Mysteries which gave them further insights and invited an even closer relationship with Demeter. Again it is secret as to how this part of the ritual was performed in the Temple and the exact nature of what was revealed remains shrouded in history.

Maybe as Aristotle wrote, the intention was "to suffer, to feel, to experience impressions and psychic moods".

Certainly it seems that in the final Fourth Triad which Demeter has given us, our "Golden Triangle", the teachings would equate with this final aspect of the Higher Initiation. We are instructed in the way of working with the higher energies of The Great Mystery, Love, Inspiration, Vision, Hope and Truth, and encouraged to explore these for ourselves. Again, her passionate commitment to free choice, and the lessons therein, is reinforced and this was very much the way of the rites at Eleusis.

We can imagine the tremendous feeling of elation and celebration amongst the Initiates at the closing festivities of the Mysteries. After an intense ten days of Sacred festival and ritual they then prepared to return to Athens in small groups over the 23rd and 24th of Boedromion.

"With the end of the celebration at Eleusis, the special obligations of the Initiates to the Sanctuary and to the Goddess came to an end. They were not obliged to return to the Sanctuary periodically to worship; they were not obligated to follow certain patterns of life or rules of conduct. They were not formed into bands or clubs dedicated to the service of the Goddess nor did they belong to what we call a "church body". They were free to return to their normal life enriched by their Eleusinian experiences which helped them to become "more pious, more just and better in everything" as Didoras states." G E Mylonas

Isn't this exactly how Demeter presents her guidance for us, that we can take it, learn from it and use it in our everyday lives? No ritual, no form of worship to a deity, just greater insight into the soul dimension and more joyous living.

"The secret of the Mysteries was kept successfully and we shall perhaps never be able to fathom it or unravel it. A thick impenetrable veil indeed still covers securely the rites of Demeter and protects them from the curious eyes of modern students." G E Mylonas

From knowing nothing of Demeter, or indeed the Great Mysteries, to being the recipient and beneficiary of what I believe to be the great wisdom teachings in her Manuscript, is in itself a mystery that I still cannot, nor indeed wish to, fathom myself. I am eternally grateful for her ongoing support and encouragement in finally bringing this manuscript, the "Revelation" of the Secretas, through the veil and into publication for the benefit of all women in today's world, that we may again learn to live and grow in the Sacred Way.

Thank you Demeter, I am honoured to have been your scribe and student.

THE CYCLE OF GROWTH AND LEARNING

The four manuscripts of Demeter, Ishtar, Mary, and Ceridwen form a whole cycle of learning and growth.

This draws on the annual physical cycle of seeding in spring, nurturing and tending through summer, harvesting in autumn, and rest and assimilating in winter, so each manuscript helps us with a facet of this in our own "metaphysical" cycle, our soul journey.

However, as they were given over a period of four years, the manuscripts may require four years or more to study and assimilate and then be worth repeating or selectively studying, for your deeper understanding and sacred life practise.

You will intuitively know exactly where you need to focus your energies for the next stage of your growth, and you will also be guided by the Goddess messengers as you begin to undertake this journey.

There are powerful threads which weave and connect our learning and life experiences in a way that only becomes apparent once we commit to work in this way.

With time and increased trust and wisdom, this interlinking of the teachings of the manuscripts enriches their context and significance, affirming their role as a part of the Mystery for your personal growth and empowerment.

The Demeter Manuscript: The Secretas of the Great Mystery

Demeter is the Initiator, the seeder, the one who introduces the concepts of our metaphysical journey, of "Soul Gardening" and The Natural Law of Returns.

Her use of simple, natural metaphors helps us easily to understand her messages and the tools she gives us with which to work our "Soul Garden" are explained gradually with natural ease and simplicity.

The Ishtar Manuscript: Jewels of the Night

Ishtar comes next with the ongoing subtle, but advanced, techniques, which we need to tend to further grow our etheric skills for inner beauty and sensuality as women. These are classic requirements in the work of the Feminine Mysteries if we are to reclaim and resurrect our Sacred Truth from the mass of misunderstandings in the Western world and its projected concept of women's roles.

She wants us to lift the veil of misunderstanding and begin to harness the true beauty of who we are.

She said, "By helping you reclaim the beauty of who you are, we reclaim the Beauty of the World".

Her "Jewels" of wisdom build on the tools that Demeter taught and then proceed to extend our understandings to allow us to work with our own thought field in a more advanced and subtle way.

She was the hardest energy to scribe as she barely had a whisper and her energy felt like gossamer silk.

I truly had to advance my own resonance and sensitivity to meet her.

Her own beauty is overwhelmingly full of power and delight.

The Mary Manuscript: Lessons for a Pure and Blessed Life

Mary of the Pure and Shining Heart arrives with great tenderness to share her lessons as we move into harvest, a time of exceptionally hard labour and focus as we gather the fruits of our soul growth.

Gently she gives practical instructions and guidance to help us stay on track and to receive our blessings.

She tells us simply,

"Deepen your connections to the Soul Level.

Open your hearts to all who suffer.

Cause no suffering yourselves.

Strengthen in the light of Great Love".

We can see her energies at work in many places of our lives where we are called as carers to practise compassion. When we are tender and open to the truth of our hearts, then we may experience tears as she encourages us to know our true natures. We fully realise that we can never hurt another without hurting ourselves. This realisation leads us home to her great gift of peace, the reward of purity in heart, mind, body, and soul.

"Call me by name when you are in need . . . . I have deep endless reserves of solace, like waves I release them in your tears. Do not be afraid to cry therefore—deep healing release."

With her help we complete the third stage of our sacred cycle.

The Ceridwen Manuscript: The Book of Ceremonies

Finally Ceridwen, the "Mystress of Ceremony", arrives to instruct us in the Sacred Arts of celebration and ceremony.

As befits an abundant harvest, there needs to be an honouring of all we have grown before we then settle down to "lay fallow" and assimilate our learning in preparation for the next time of seeding.

"Sharing that which is Sacred in Life, on Feast Days, on Grief Days, at Procession times, this keeps community healthy".

This manuscript is a vital tool for any Celebrant who is working with community ceremonies but also includes a vital section on the need for personal sacred ceremonies.

Now it is time to rest and reflect, to deepen the awareness of your soul journey, and to make adjustments where things are now outdated because you have changed or because they are no longer relevant in our lives.

It naturally fosters another season of "letting go".

So we complete our cycle of metaphysical growth and learning with a period of stillness, our winter before the new season of seeding in spring, when we have to dig the soil/soul and prepare it for our new cycle of growth.

The timing at which you choose to start your cycle of learning and growth will naturally need to allow for personal variations, especially between northern and southern hemispheres.

I have started in September here in Australia in line with the original festival of Demeter (autumn in Greece/spring in Australia), and I have started in March (autumn here in Australia/ spring in Europe). Both timings have been effective.

If you are working alone, you may choose to start after a birthday or significant personal milestone.

With a group, it may work best to run the gatherings within the natural calendar year from January to December.

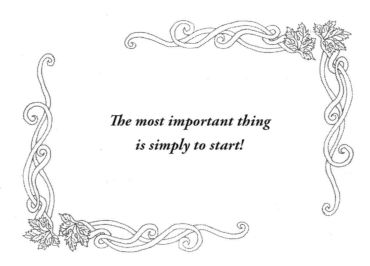

*The most important thing
is simply to start!*

CREATING A SACRED CIRCLE

How to share the Demeter Manuscript in a Sacred Circle way

When I had received the full *Demeter Manuscript* of teachings, I was quite honestly so overwhelmed that I needed an "outside" opinion so I took them to a friend, Paula Milner. Paula ran The Cottage Retreat in Boome, a place where I, and other healers and spiritual seekers, gathered regularly for meditation, workshops, and general sharing "get-togethers".

Paula generously suggested we offer a workshop to trial the teachings.

I sat with this and felt very strongly that it needed to cover a full year in time to allow for the changes which I felt sure would follow.

So that is what we did.

We met once a month in 2001 and carefully studied each teaching, using many other tools to assist us, such as journaling, art, dance, and music . . . Yes we had great fun as well as many tears of relief and healing!

From this I learnt of the need to create a Sacred Space where the women could feel safe, and so the notion of forming a Sacred Circle began.

This is the form I have used ever since, and of course each group of women has been different, but each has been equally beautiful and brilliant in the way they have learnt to honour themselves and each other as Sacred Soul beings.

It is like watching the lotus blossom open to the rays of the sunshine as each woman unfolds that potential which she contains as her birthright and releases the restrictions on her soul, which have been cramping and limiting her natural beauty and fragrance.

If you feel drawn to sharing the teachings in this way, then I can offer you some guidelines on establishing and maintaining a Sacred Circle. You will receive many blessings for this work, I can assure you.

I can also offer you the back-up of *The Sacred Journal: Soul Gardening,* which contains my collection of reflections and suggestions for activities to help you and your group as you work through *The Demeter Manuscript.*

First of all though, you really need to have experience and familiarity with the nature of the manuscript and the teachings for yourself.

When you feel comfortable, then here are the guidelines that I can simply recommend for this Sacred Circle Work.

1. Be clear in your intention, and know that you are working not for money but for the Blessing of the Goddess and her abundant gifts in your life. The girls I have gathered with have always wanted to make a donation, so this has been welcomed and then used to cover any costs. Sometimes we have chosen to donate the balance to help a local or favourite charitable cause.

2. Start talking about your intention, and gather some friends and women who might wish to share in a "Sacred Circle" of growth and learning. Explain about the teachings of Demeter and how they seed a wonderful year of transformation.

3. Find a "Sacred Space" where you can feel secure and welcome, so that you can all relax and share. I love to use my own home and garden as a base.

4. Set a time and a date. The beginning of the year is always good but by no means necessary. I have found that evenings suit women who work or mums who have a co-operative partner, friend, or family member who can care for their children, whilst the weekend can work once in a while but not on a regular basis throughout the full year.

5. Hold an information and sharing session first. It is essential to outline the requirements for Sacred Circle work, as it is not like any other group that comes together socially. Some women may not feel comfortable in a group and prefer to study alone. However, the group synergy really creates a dimension that helps the growth and discovery of all the participants.

    I always start around the table, with a central candle and flowers or other natural elements. We hold hands, close our eyes, and are present with each other, and then

share a blessing. We may use this time to send healing energy to anyone or anywhere in the planet where it is needed. We also close in a similar way before the circle is broken.

6. Explain the need for total confidentiality within the group. This is a fundamental prerequisite as without this, women will not allow themselves to fully open. I describe it as a sisterhood: no gossip, no judgement, no criticism. Simply pure acceptance of each other as a circle of souls who are learning to trust and value each other without any sense of needing to compete. This is the whole point of "sacred".

7. Introduce the concept of talking and listening in circle. Each woman needs to be heard so that when she talks she is received fully and not interrupted. Using a "talking stick" or totem is a useful way to hold respect for the speaker. The practise of "active listening" is essential as a skill to support each other with full attention and respect. There is an initial tendency for women to try to offer advice and solve the problems of others, but unless this is invited by the speaker, then it is not a part of this way of listening and working in circle.

8. Make it clear that each woman has gifts that she can bring to the group and share. These may not be evident initially but will emerge throughout the journey of the year. Creating an atmosphere of individual appreciation and encouragement within the group enriches the diversity of the gatherings and acts as an inspiration to others.

9. Decide if you want to include food as a part of the circle gathering. At first I felt it was my responsibility to provide refreshments for everyone, but since then I have invited a "bring and share" approach that has resulted in some evenings of absolute feast. There will always be a "foodie" or two ready to delight the taste buds or someone who wants to share a new or favourite recipe. This would be my recommended way! The "girls" love it, and it adds another dimension to the whole feeling of celebrating with Demeter.

10. Finally, introduce and welcome your teacher, Demeter, and explain that each month you will be sharing one of her Secretas, and that there will be "homework." Make sure everyone has a copy of *The Sacred Mystery Manuscripts,* which includes in full *The Demeter Manuscript, and the Sacred Journal* that they have agreed to the dates and put them in their diary (their commitment is to themselves so expect full attendance as they realise their inner need for soul nurturing), and start looking forward to a fabulous year in your life.

Another beautiful friend, Lynn Webb from my old hometown of Narrogin in the wheat-belt area of SW Australia, has also run circles using the Demeter teachings. Here are some of her suggestions and reflections.

"The forming of a circle is one of the most life-changing experiences we as women can experience; with the added focus of these manuscripts, it can be nothing less than profound.

When we as individuals began to unfold separately and explore these messages monthly in our daily experience of life, much wisdom and personal understanding was gained. One of the most profound learnings was how deeply connected we really are. As we came back each month to share, we were but a mirror for each other. What a safe place it was to be vulnerable, to be supported, to be held when in despair, and to learn to hold others in their great times of learning.

As we explored our dreams and allowed ourselves to dream the biggest dream, there have been many Dreams that have been realised, and the Creative force has exploded among us. There is awesome power in unleashing one's highest potential.

Above all, this journey has been Joyful, filled with much Love, Connection, and Learning. It is with deep Love and Gratitude that I recommend Journeying with these manuscripts.

My only suggestion is that each group allow for Demeter's energy to direct the group, as I have found that no two groups are the same. The work does what it needs to do. Some like to have a Leader or something more formal in place; others prefer it be more spontaneous in nature and presentation.

The most important thing is that all participants make it a Sacred and Safe place for deep, heart-centred sharing and that each evening there is a practise that connects everyone into such an energy.

Either a meditation is used, a piece of inspirational song/ music, a ritual or prayer, a poem or any other practise desired.

We would begin each evening by taking it in turns around the Circle, reading the Secreta for the Month's focus, followed by a discussion regarding the content. We would share within the group any Wisdom we had on the subject, any Fear that we had rising or issues we had around the homework. For the next Month, we would review and devote our focus to one lesson, taking notes as events unfolded for us within our day-to-day lives. Even if we didn't get around to doing the homework, we found that during our sharing we could gain insight into what stopped us from doing so.

In one group, we have taken it in turns to provide and share a beautiful monthly meal, with others we have had a cuppa and nibbles/biscuits, etc. All have been suitable to the needs and requirements of each group.

In the "busy-ness" of daily life, finding a suitable night proved to be the most difficult thing so I found it easier to make the meeting date coincide with each Full Moon. The feedback from this has been profound, as even if someone is unable to attend one month, seeing the full moon connects her into the group anyway. You will find that attendance will be pretty much 100 percent as it becomes something you just don't want to miss; it is the greatest appointment you can have with yourself!

Wishing you a Wonderful Journey.

Enjoy your unfolding as you blossom, and embrace the magnificent energy of the Sacred Goddess energy."

Namaste,
Lynn Webb, Narrogin, WA

JOINING THE GLOBAL CIRCLE

Your Global Connection and Power through Demeter

As we work to transform ourselves and align ourselves with the Cosmic Soul, we join and help create a huge web of light that is changing our whole way of being human.

The tools of practise for our Sacred journey, which Demeter outlines, naturally begin to change the way in which we live our lives, the way we make choices, the way we take personal responsibility and exercise our power.

This cannot help but have a vital impact on our immediate families and circle of friends, and then our wider community.

Probably the most extensive potential shift is for our own children, the future of our planet.

As we become increasingly conscious of our personal Soul Garden, we gently begin to allow this consciousness to enter our homes, our relationships, and our child rearing practices.

To begin to raise children with an awareness of "Soul" outside of any ritual or prescriptive religious dogma is a powerful force that links them across the globe with a higher consciousness.

At the moment, I am beginning to write what I feel needs to be a practical guide for spirituality and soul consciousness within the family, in order to help bring through this natural wisdom for children on a very simple home-based level.

Harnessing the source of power within is surely a smart way to help lift the world's resonance whilst developing and retaining a sense of personal value and fulfilment, which is authentic and beyond the temporary gratifications of external or material status.

I believe that "soul hunger", and in some cases "soul starvation" or "spiritual bankruptcy", is the greatest source of illness today, especially in the fields of depression and other mental illnesses, which we know are increasing at an alarming rate. Demeter even mentions suicide as she talks

about the "crushed souls who have ceased to find a way to breathe life into their dreams", in the Eighth Secreta.

We cannot begin to know quite how we might impact on this in a global way, but for myself, I can see that the tools have helped me to grow through my own "dark night of the Soul", seeking deeply to find the soul lessons from the many human challenges which seemed to present as a big basket of "lemons" for the last few years! (The final "lemon" being when our beloved dog Tessie died. A fun-loving springer spaniel and sensitive companion for many happy years, I was totally bereft and poured an ocean of grief and tears over her final rite of passage.)

I feel they have helped me to stay strong in my search for spiritual meaning and inner truth, especially on those difficult occasions when I feel I would previously have struggled with trying to reason and understand.

Accepting the need for "good grief" and deeper compassion, learning to let go in love, and permitting myself to move on have been additional blessings.

Knowing that I am never alone, and actually feeling the gentle but powerful way that I am helped whenever I ask, has enriched my understanding of my soul connection and my ability to trust and surrender to this wonderful source of Great Love.

In itself, this has a value far beyond anything I can measure and yet again affirms the power of these teachings.

I can recommend them to anyone who is being challenged as a parent, a mother, a lover, a wife, a sister, a daughter, a girlfriend, a woman, a human.

This is the journey the world needs us to take, as holders of the Sacred Feminine Soul, as women of wholeness who can embrace the magnificent value of life's challenges, of our imperfections, and mistakes, as opposed to the "sin" and subsequent guilt with which we have been shackled.

We are after all, the chief holders of the "Recipe for Lemonade".

The Imperfection is the Perfection.

Embracing the journey to the Sacred in the way that Demeter outlines and becoming "Soul Gardeners" links us with a beautiful ancient source in Spirit and also with other global Soul Gardeners in the spiral that never ends.

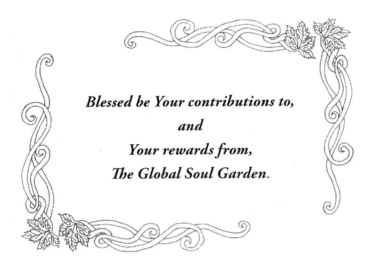

Blessed be Your contributions to,
and
Your rewards from,
The Global Soul Garden.

THE DEMETER GIRLS SHARE THEIR STORIES

The greatest tribute that I can pay to these teachings from Demeter is to have the privilege of sharing some of the feelings and feedback from a few of the *girls* who have taken the full year to work through the manuscript and rethink their roles as women.

With the support of a group, or on their own, they have had the courage to get "down and dirty" in the core of their Soul Gardening and make the changes to their lives that have enriched them and created true fulfilment.

Thank you girls, for sharing these stories from your hearts.

My life's journey has been blessed by you all.

May these affirmations inspire women the world over to become "Soul Gardeners", to grow and flourish within themselves as beautiful fruits and flowers in this our wonderful, Sacred garden of Planet Earth.

We start with Kylie, a passionate early childhood teacher and a member of the first Demeter circle in Broome.

> I feel truly blessed to have been able to have an encounter with Demeter. I have learnt so much more about myself through the teachings of the Great Mystery.
>
> I feel very fortunate to have had this wonderful encounter at such a difficult time in my life. It was almost ten years ago, and I was pregnant with my son, feeling very uncertain about the future as I was soon to become a sole parent without a lot of family support around me. I remember the Demeter workshops with such fondness because they truly did empower me, and I began to feel blessed that I was carrying new life, rather than fearing the impending birth and the unknown.

I truly do feel that I began to grow. I remember doing the tree of life and the symbols that I drew back then have come to fruition now. I have a loving partner with three beautiful children. I am living by the beach, and I am happy!

After each workshop with Demeter, I used to feel so euphoric! It was as if everything made sense. It also helped me to understand my feelings of grief from the loss of my own mother at a young age. I would often get goosebumps and tingles when we would receive a blessing. I remember feeling a lot of Love. To this day, I re-read her words and still gain so much. I thank you Tricia for this wonderful encounter, and to Demeter of course!

Kylie Stott, NSW

Possibly the most poignant reflection on the teachings comes from Katrina, a young mother who joined our first group knowing she had been diagnosed with a potentially terminal condition. Her bravery was an inspiration to us all.

What a year! I look at the poster of Demeter and I see the nurturer, the mother caring for us all so we can reach our full potential.

The year has been for me a year of spiritual development. Because of Demeter and my illness, I have slowed down and am taking more time to observe nature, learning to enjoy what is around me. I have developed more patience with my family and send love to difficult situations. I feel my illness is a part of healing myself so that I can love myself.

Highlights of the Demeter gatherings were activities such as dancing in the cottage where I felt the spiritual connection of my essence and protection from my guardian angel. I enjoyed drawing the tree of life with my aspirations for the future, which was the picture of my beautiful garden where I enjoy meditational bliss. The dancing around the rock of course was total freedom (*at the women's Sacred space of Riddell Beach in Broome*).

Self-realisations (the raised self-awareness that occurred throughout the Demeter year) were about being gentle with myself and that anything else is an illusion.

The Fifth Secreta of Silence has for myself brought about bliss through meditation. The bliss only lasts for a few seconds and not every day, but hopefully this will be developed.

The Sixth Secreta of Being Alone had the success for myself of letting go of fear. Demeter stated, "Let your fears blow away with the wind because you no longer need them to restrict you". I don't know whether I have reached this point as yet, but I have come a long way.

The Ninth Secreta, of the dark side part of my life's journey, will hopefully help me learn the lessons from this illness to let go of my fears by accepting All That Is. I get great comfort when Demeter states that love is the life force. It is a source of joy and healing for me.

Later in her lessons, she states, "And be in your heart-full place for your truth to shine as an example for those around you".

I want to shine for my children. My children are the seeds I have put on Earth, and I love watching them grow so they can reach their full potential.

Thank you, Tricia and Paula, for giving me the opportunity to experience Demeter. Thank you to all the other beautiful ladies who shared the Demeter nights with me.

Katrina, Broome

Blessings and thanks, Katrina, now in Spirit, but a beautiful teacher for us all as she allowed us to be a part of her soul journey.

Next we have Paula, my friend from Broome, Reiki master, Aura Soma teacher, grandmother, and wise woman of many other gifts.

On reflection of The Sacred Goddess Manuscripts, Demeter, Ishtar, Mary, and Ceridwen, I am reminded of the abundant gift of knowledge and wisdom given to Tricia to share with a lucky few of us in 2001.

It is amazing to realise that it is over ten years ago now since the first of the manuscripts, that of Demeter, was shared with the first group of women, in circle, at my Cottage Retreat in Broome, and that of course this ancient knowledge is still as valid now as it was then,

By the time the Mary manuscript had been scribed, Tricia was moving to the south-west, so I was privileged to be offered the opportunity to present this wisdom. So it was that Mary's "Lessons for Pure and Blessed Life" became the central teaching in my course of "Sacred Circles," to a second group of ten wonderful women.

This was a series of ten weekly gatherings to explore many tools to enhance intuitive development, and also ideas to find positive and creative ways towards personal growth and the clearing away of old patterns.

Mary asked of us to understand that "Peace arises from each of us in a spirit of Love."

Needless to say, transformation happened for each of us in many ways within that circle.

Paula Milner, WA

Here then a variety of other personal reflections from just some of the beautiful women who have taken the time to listen to, and work with, Demeter.

I personally have grown in so many ways (that I didn't even know were possible) as I have absorbed each Secreta along this twelve-month journey and beyond!

Naively, I believed I didn't have any issues to deal with. After all, I have a healthy marriage, two beautiful children, and an insatiable drive to fulfil my time, every waking moment! Always more plans and projects than would prove possible to accomplish in one lifetime . . .

And then I discovered *me!*

I realised how satisfying time alone could be, focused contemplation and Soul Gardening. A huge wave of patience, change of pace, and taking time out to literally smell the roses or banksias in my garden, appreciating all the little things that eventually weave together into the truly beautiful *big* picture/blanket/mosaic of my Life.

I began to put myself first above the role of wife, mother, or friend. I have a wonderful (*and much used*) ear, but I have learnt to not hold the negativity from others and allow it to be moved on healthily.

I have always believed that if you want something badly enough, you will get it. Through Demeter and the truly special circle of friends, I have gained the tools to help make all my dreams come true.

With sincere thanks and blessings,

"Goddess Sarah," WA

I have been privileged to have been part of a group of women who have met monthly and read and shared experiences from *The Demeter Manuscript.*

It has been one of the most profound and moving times in my life. I have had my eyes opened to much of my "stuff" with this support. I would encourage anyone to read and explore these teachings.

Bev McMillan, WA

I am happy to sing the praises of Demeter. She represents to the women of today a "Modern Goddess Guide" whose teachings can be implemented on a daily, yearly, or continuous cycle for life. I often refer to her words even a year on, and I will continue to do so.

Lynn Elliot, WA

The journey for me was life changing. Not only did I learn of love and laughter, there were tears as well as I learnt to deal with some ghost buried deep down as well as fears and self-doubt. We were guided each month not only with how to face these challenges, but how to come out the other side with a confidence so strong I can't put it into words. Knowing I am not alone in my journey through life is a great comfort to me! I can say without a doubt that if I had not taken this journey with Demeter, I would no longer be married. Through the work I did with Demeter, I not only healed myself as a woman, but saved my marriage and, through that, my two beautiful children also benefited.

On the light side of things, it was so much fun meeting with our group of girls each month, just sharing events and hearing about others in return. Having a voice that gets heard in a positive light and getting a positive response back made a difference to me.

The release that talking and dancing around a fire can give is amazing. I learnt to skip like a child without a care in the world, to feel free of my daily worries, not only getting me through my week but empowering me for my whole life!

What a gift—time to just be you!

Who thought meeting just one "Goddess" could change your life so much?

So, open your heart to Demeter and allow her love to heal and guide you. It will be the best gift you have ever received.

Thank you Tricia, for the journey and for introducing me to Demeter.

Susan, WA

It is with great pleasure that I recommend these manuscripts by Tricia Mary Lee.

The teachings can at first appear to be almost too simple, too practical, and we can believe there is nothing new in this material. In a sense this is true; we have heard it all before in many different ways, books, and programs. However, when

a group of woman is called together, with these manuscripts as a focus, there is a great deal of magic that comes with it.

When Tricia first asked me to read these manuscripts, I must admit to at first being blind to the power of the energy. At the time, I was deeply involved in my own spiritual journey and practices, and I found these Secretas to be almost repetitive in nature, of much in the "New Age" material that had been surfacing in the years preceding the arrival of Demeter.

However, almost as a favour to Tricia, I decided that it would be great to form a group and work with the manuscript, and so began a most wonderful Journey, one that I am deeply grateful to have been inspired to be involved in.

Lynn Webb, WA

When I started working with *The Demeter Manuscript,* I had just left my eighteen-year marriage. I was not able to bring myself to join the group who were starting so I chose to do this by myself with the help of Tricia.

I took the time to do this when I felt the need. Sometimes I'd go through a couple of chapters then go back and revisit some chapters.

I had a lot of trouble with silence, but now, two and a half years later, I can enjoy silence. I had never spent time alone, and now I enjoy that as well. I never was able to save money, and I never had any spare. It took a while, but now I always have enough for what I need, and I have created a lovely home so that my kids have not missed out on anything.

I also have wonderful friends and a great job in my life. Initially I thought that I wouldn't be able to cope on my own, but now I am very independent and capable.

One night after asking my friends if they would come to a show with me and they had other things planned, I decided to go by myself. I drove 130 kilometres to see the show and drove home again, not once feeling scared or alone. I was so proud of myself and enjoyed the show immensely.

I have really grown as a woman and as a person through working with these teachings.

Thank you to Tricia and Demeter.

Karen Fox, WA

I was at an aimless end when Demeter with her timely wisdom came along. It wasn't just the insights and suggestions, but also the sharing amongst the group that was extremely valuable. My personal favourite was the Orhiba (*Health Exercise routine from Indonesia which is great as a morning energy alignment, if possible outdoors*). Celebrating our kind universe and our own greatness, along with meditation, instilled a sense of oneness. I'm extremely grateful for the generosity of everyone in the group whilst we were sharing the insights, for Tricia's generous introduction to all these great gifts of forgotten memories and wisdom, and also for the love and hospitality she and John share.

Lots of love,
Anne Kennedy McGee, WA

I have, through following these teachings and accepting the life experiences which have surrounded them, felt a sense of "training" in my spiritual pathway This combines a sense of awareness and growth that seems to honour and teach me through my life as a woman, not as an aesthete on retreat, nor as a nun or monk in a mountain cave somewhere, but fully in the presence of my active role as wife, mother, daughter, sister, aunty, woman.

I increasingly feel an organic connection with the miracle of spiritual embodiment manifested through my daily routines with the ordinary work of cooking, cleaning, caring, shopping, gardening, sewing, mending, and all the other domestic necessities of keeping home.

Inducted also by the Goddess messengers into the Sacred Healing Arts, from sacred dance to song writing, from painting to performing, from love making to

music making, from tender fragrant massage to silent meditation, the therapeutic power of the creative force has woven its way endlessly in, around, and through my Sacred feminine soul.

It seems as if the whole essence of the Sacred Mystery has infused and transformed my way of being a woman. I realise that the closer I am to my soul's way of being, the nearer I need to be to the Earth's soil, as if the natural order has a vital place for me to be safe and sustained amidst what can seem like a chaotic, turbulent world.

I consider myself a woman of many blessings and give great thanks to all my teachers in Spirit and also those around me here as I work to live gently and playfully, day by day.

Blessed Be,
Tricia Mary Lee, WA

As you can see, there has been a huge range of different comments, feelings, and results from those taking this year with Demeter, but for me, one abiding feeling is present in all these responses and that is one of total gratitude, thankfulness for the unique growth and learning that has occurred in relation to the different needs of each individual woman, each one reflecting a separate facet of the beauty of the Great Mother Energy.

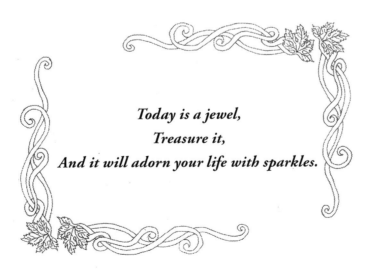

Today is a jewel,
Treasure it,
And it will adorn your life with sparkles.

THE PATH OF THE MODERN PRIESTESS

Any work with the Goddess inevitably leads to a discussion of the role of the Priestess. We know of the honoured rites of the Priestess in ancient cultures and religious traditions, but where is she today?

If you, like me, are a woman and, then you are probably one of the many searching, also like me, to find a way to bring about change, to connect with a deep and hungry longing for a better way of being human, to answer a call which is gathering voice and which urges us to respond from the truest knowing of our hearts.

Traditionally, a Priestess "ministered" to her family and her community in the ways of the Goddess, Sacred Mother or Great Mystery. She was the one who had been trained in the Sacred Arts and who held the gifts of wisdom, insight, prophecy, and natural healing.

With the last two thousand years of Western patriarchal religions, the role of the Priestess has been virtually buried, but with the powerful incoming tide of the Aquarian energy, her role is being called forth as both an archetype and as a practical manifestation, from the depths of our global soul.

As an archetype, symbolically the Priestess stands as the gatekeeper between the Earth and the Heavens, as the holder of the veil that separates all things unseen in the Mystery from all things of the flesh on Earth.

She comes in dreams, and visions in answer to our inner quest for sacred feminine wisdom and understanding.

She holds the key of *communion* (meaning "union with" or "as one") with the Sacred (that which is *secret* or beyond the veil) through her advanced abilities to receive guidance from the high Feminine energies that lie beyond the physical human realm.

In the outer practical reality, she represents their wishes for wholeness through her healing and teaching work with the people of the Earth. (In techno speak, she is the receptor and converter of

the waves of energy which we can all download into our thought field to inform our behaviours and our actions.)

There are so many stories and legends, myths and mysteries surrounding the role of the Priestess in ancient history that we can draw on. Across the Egyptian, Greek, Roman, Celtic, Mayan, and other ancient cultures, we can access insights, but our quest today, when we are advancing into a global community (i.e., with unity or union), starts by asking, "What does a modern Priestess for the twenty-first century look like?"

How does she proceed in modern countries that now span a myriad of ancient and modern cultures, and where the emancipation of women seems manifest in the realms of education, politics, health, and work opportunities but still clearly not in the sphere of religion?

Where is her "temple" in the paradox of a society like Australia, which still holds the indigenous understanding of the land as Sacred against the imposed Western notion of the need for a bricks-and-mortar church, along with the title of a certain group or formal denomination?

Why do we need the Priestess? Why here, or in Europe and America?

If you feel that you are being "called" to journey on this pathway, then her Great Mystery is already at work, and you will certainly be wondering about your responses.

Here are several contemporary "portraits" of women which point to how she might look.

- She is a daughter, sister, wife, mother, grandmother, or aunty. She already shares her life with other women, and possibly men, from the perspective of her experiences as a woman. She is familiar with the emotional tides that tug on her heart during the menstrual and moon cycles, and she feels connected to the natural flow of creativity and reproduction. She understands the vital power of water and respects her own inner needs for both stillness and wilderness. She can embrace chaos as a source of change and transformation and yet can create order through her understanding of the traditional rites of passage.
- She is engaged in a caring, counselling or therapeutic role within her family or local community. She has chosen to learn, share, and practise the arts of compassion and tenderness for those who are weaker or less able in our society. She may be drawn to help with terminal care and the final rite of passage as a "soul companion." She is able

to honour her own sense of "the imperfection is the perfection" and has assimilated the Law of Natural Returns (*The Demeter Manuscript*).

- She is trained in one of the many wonderful natural healing modalities that have escalated into mainstream consciousness over the last twenty to thirty years. From bodywork to natural remedies, there is now a feast of options to support her holistically in her journey and to empower her in her choices of natural remedies over pharmaceutical drugs. She realises that her health is of greater value than her wealth and promotes a pure and healthy lifestyle by her own example.

- She is interested in learning how she can live with a cleaner, greener footprint and is trying to incorporate this as a lifestyle choice. She may be a keen gardener or may even be connected with the environmental sustainability industry or the land-care and organic foods movement. She values the quality of her environment and identifies with it as an aspect of herself.

- She is exploring, or working through, the therapeutic healing or entertainment arts of dance and movement, music and song, or the visual, literary, theatre, or media arts. Her urge to explore and express herself sensually and artistically is an intrinsic and vital part of her well-being. Her sense of inner and outer beauty creates a radiance that enhances the world around her *(The Ishtar Manuscript: Jewels of the Night)*. Equally, she encourages others in their own creative arts pursuits and leads or supports community development in the arts.

- She is committed to the promotion of healthy eating and takes pleasure in sharing the experience of preparing and cooking fine-quality food and drink for her family and friends. She tries to grow some of her own foods and shops carefully for natural and local produce.

- She is an avid recycler. From compost to clothes, she likes to convert waste into fertiliser and uses her imagination and dedication to create new for old. She is a ready student of "Soul Gardening" *(The Demeter Manuscript: The Secretas of the Great Mystery)* and seeks to work organically with her inner and outer life.

- She is an ongoing student of the different ways of culture and spirituality. Her personal practise may draw upon a range of tools and strategies which she has found to work for herself and which may vary, depending on the age and stage of life at which she finds herself, rather like the way that dietary needs differ from children to pensioners. She recognises her own need for "soul food" or spiritual sustenance but has also realised that her vitality of life force comes from an alignment to something she cannot define and which is strengthened through her links to the wider community.

- She is a lover of auspicious ceremony. She may be a trained Celebrant or an unofficial "Mystress of Ceremonies" *(The Ceridwen Manuscript: The Book of Ceremonies)*. She seeks to enrich her life and that of those around her with personalised ceremonies of heartfelt meaning. She feels comfortable working from the heart and aims to reflect that in her planning and preparation of special events to mark the passage time in the lives of her family and community and to celebrate the fullness of the life cycle from birth to death.

- She is, above all, committed with a passion to Peace and seeks to create her own life of blessings amidst the turmoil that may sometimes present itself at her door. *(The Mary Manuscript: Lessons for a Pure and Blessed Life)*. She acts as a "midwife" for the birth of a new generation of thoughts and behaviours which are transcending the ego limitations of humanity, thereby transforming the consciousness of Planet Earth.

So, does any of this sound like you or some of your recent life's journey?

Welcome to the Path of the Modern Priestess.

Proceeding to the next stage of this path involves a move in consciousness.

It seems to be the natural way in all things, that first we commit to our heart's intention, then we work to plant the seed and nurture it before we can finally harvest the fruits and have something of value to share with our community.

Traditionally, a Priestess committed fully to her spiritual pathway of service through her training and initiation, the taking of her vows, and then her ordination. Perhaps this next step of intention is for you.

A vow is a powerful resolution that is made as a sign of readiness to enter into conscious and willing partnership with the Sacred Feminine Mystery.

It is a declaration which is based on the recognition of your connection with a greater source of wisdom.

It is at one and the same time a simple measure of trust, surrender, and empowerment.

This in itself is a Sacred contract, which you make when you are ready to commit your heart, mind, body, and soul to the spiritual journey of conscious, hands-on service.

And what about your temple?

Your feminine body is your Sacred temple for this work, and the creation of your inner temple allows for your heart to fully open so that you can receive directly the wishes and insights that will inspire you and guide you in your outer work. The community of family and friends around you is your direct concern and, through their well-being and growth, you will achieve an ever circling impact of change without need for a single sermon!

Why here?

Why now?

I believe we are seeding here in Australia (and in cultures across the globe) the spiritual future of our children in a global society. The opportunities to transform the way of the World to a purer, healthier, more natural, and more loving way of being are enormous.

In a way, I feel we in Australia hold the last chance for a better way of being, as a "new and old" society that is bringing together the ancient indigenous and the modern Western worlds.

In this process, in this place where the sacred rituals for the Earth, our Soul soil, are still honoured, we are reclaiming the Feminine body as Sacred.

In doing this, we are releasing, on a deep, cellular level, any past associations with sexual or bodily guilt that have lodged in the feminine organs of breasts, ovaries, and uterus, manifesting in the illnesses we see for women of today.

The final emancipation of women lies in our freedom to celebrate our inner Sacred essence in our direct relationship with the Mystery as co-creators and organic facets of one and the same life force.

With a network of such "Community Priestesses" in Australia and other modern countries, we have a quiet, dynamic, spiritual pathway for hands-on wholeness and "Soul-driven" transformation.

As an additional part of this, the natural timing of ceremonies and celebrations can then be readjusted to reflect our southern hemisphere seasons.

For Easter and new life in spring, we can look to September, for growth and flowering in summer we reach December, for reaping in harvest in autumn we arrive in March, and for drawing in the light in midwinter we celebrate in June/July. We cannot in Australia continue to blindly celebrate rituals from the imported Christian church, which are obviously based on the calendar of the northern hemisphere, in such a way that diminishes the authentic and original meaning of our spiritual and seasonal rhythm of festivities.

A community calendar of local food and Earth-based celebrations soon creates a more appropriate and healthier alternative as a starting point. Every Priestess has a role here!

So, be welcome to the "Path of the Modern Priestess", she who is empowered, through her Sacred feminine wisdom, to grow herself and her world in beauty, love, and blessings from the original intention that is planted in her Sacred soul as her Divine birthright.

May your journey home be blessed
With the wonder of a child's eyes
and the courage of a lioness,
With the radiance of the full moon
and the fragrance of the sun-kissed rose.

Soul Gardening with Demeter

CREATING YOUR SACRED JOURNAL

elcome . . .

This journal is a beautiful, important and precious part of your Sacred journey this year with Demeter.

As a sign of your preparation and personal intent, it is wonderful to create your own personalised cover.

An A4 ring binder file is an ideal way of keeping everything together, but making it special for you, representing the sacred things in your life, creates a space that feels honoured and worthy of your deepest and innermost longings.

This is a lifelong journal so you want to make it sturdy and strong.

Here are a few suggestions for starting your creative talents flowing.

- Make a fabric cover: Paint it, use beads, sequins, jewels, embroidery, quilting, crazy patchwork . . . Use your needlework skills and imagination then stitch it to slip over the file.
- Make a collage directly onto the file: Cover it with layers of fine tissue paper and thin glue, and then add a string design or papier-mâché to raise the surface. Cover with more tissue, glue, and then paint. Add beads, shells, mirrors, fabric, anything gloriously colourful and sparkly! Cover it with glue that dries clear to protect it. Bring your inner artist out to play.
- Use Decoupage: Collect photos and pictures of favourite places, people, events, and things. Cut creatively and glue securely onto the file in a random design. Decorate with extras to make a kaleidoscope of treasures. Varnish or cover with glue that dries clear to protect it.
- Draw and paint a design: Use thick paper or card as a base for your drawing and painting. Add words or pieces of poetry that touch your heart, or add texture with

other materials. Glue the card directly onto the file with strong glue. Allow the colours of the spectrum to reflect your inner jewels.

- Choose a theme: look to nature, the landscape, plants, and animals, the seasons, the sun, moon, and stars, the elements of fire, Earth, water, air, the kingdom of devas, a labyrinth or anything which inspires or is symbolic for you. Start creating from your beautiful soul space now.

PREPARING A SACRED TIME AND SPACE

The preparation of time and space for your *Sacred Journal* work signals your intention by moving your energy into practical action.

There are many ways to "make time" so look at your diary, your daily, weekly, monthly schedule, and see just where you are going to write in "My Sacred Time".

Once it is entered, it is an appointment which is equal to, if not more important than, the dentist, the school sports carnival, the dog-training class, the gym or aerobics circuit, or whatever other marvellous activities you use to fill your time.

This is about your soul's health and well-being.

If you are part of a group, then committing the time to join the group sessions is probably easy because it will mean you leave your house, but if you are working on this alone, then that same time commitment to read and reflect on the Secreta for that month, as well as time to journal and do the "homework," needs to be allocated.

This is where creating a Sacred space for yourself within your home, or garden, is a real support and ultimate blessing for you. It not only gives you permission to stop and think, it also delineates an invisible boundary which says, "Let go, and allow yourself to enter the Sacred space of your soul. Open to the divine connection, and be inspired".

It may be just a corner, which is quiet, or you may have a whole separate "room", either in or out of doors. Be sure you have somewhere comfy to sit and write.

Make it special with your very own touches and design. Again, allow your creativity to emerge and lead you in what feels right for you.

Representing the elements symbolically invites a strong connection with the Earth, which somehow seems fitting for "Soul Gardening".

- For fire: a candle, light, or solar lamp, the sun, incense, a fire pit
- For water: a bowl of water with flowers or shells, a water feature like a fountain or pool, a lake or pond, mirrors
- For air: wind chimes, streamers with bells, silk veils, feathers, a flag, butterflies
- For Earth: rocks, crystals or pebbles, flowers or herbs, trees or shrubs, foods

You may also want music or an instrument that you can play and space to dance, do Tai Chi or yoga. Like you, this space is flexible, dynamic, and open to new ideas and inspirations. It can delight the senses and intoxicate the heart with beauty.

Enjoy creating!

Naturally, if you have children, they will be curious about what you are doing and may want to create a space for themselves. This is wonderful and an invitation for you to share. I call this simply a "Contemplation Corner" or wilderness garden, somewhere for them to enjoy nature, stillness, silence, and time to themselves away from TV, computers, and technology.

This is especially needed for the higher-resonance star children who are now incarnating.

JOURNALING WITH DEMETER

The process of writing and journaling creates an opening to our inner temple.

As we give form to our thoughts, ideas, and reflections, so we delve deeper into our reasons, our underlying beliefs, and our core thoughts, about who, why, and how we are at this amazing point in time, here on Planet Earth.

Our ability to understand, accept, and embrace ourselves expands as we begin to let the light into our darker spaces.

As we write from our true and authentic heart, so we learn to honour and respect all aspects of ourselves as vital to our whole.

This is about revealing our metaphysical garden, not about a supermarket stocktake!

Have fun with your journal; be outrageous, bold, daring, shy, timid, and afraid—be all things as you own them to be a part of you.

The use of symbolic language, through drawing and the use of colours, is great for kids and for us too! It can enhance our enjoyment of journaling and provide a hidden dimension to what we really feel. Having the courage to express ourselves is empowering and uplifting.

Work with big paper, bold pastels, fabrics, textures, small paper, delicate watercolours, pencils, and charcoal.

Experiment with water, ink, glues, dyes, waxes, and heat.

Look for what lies underneath, what is revealed in the layers of your artworks. This gives clues to what is Sacred for You.

There is another way of being,
Another way of seeing . . . .
Together we must come for this planetary healing
In our hearts
A seed of Love
Can grow and flower big enough
To share with others round this earth
Our Mother wishes this rebirth
Are you ready for this journey home to Love?

THE FIRST SECRETA: TIME

Begin in your quiet sacred space as you wish to reflect on this first simple, but powerful teaching for this month. Time of course is a major issue for all of us with the speed of technology and the distance from the essence of our natural rhythms and seasons. However, we all do have the same number of hours in a day, days in a week, and weeks in a year. So, it is all about the choices we make within this framework and how they give an insight into the truth of our deeper selves.

How can you give yourself the gift of time?

Is there anything that you would like to change or release that you feel would make your life easier?

Which simple pleasures would you like to appreciate more?

What kind of *welcome* do you give yourself when you come home?

How can you celebrate *your* time?

In preparing for Sacred time and space, what has been the hardest part for you?

What learning do you wish to share?

This Moon . . .

This month look for different ways to clear out and make space and time in your life.

Clear out the clutter on every level. Here are some ideas to get you started . . .

- Give away old clothes, books, household items, etc. to the local charity shops.
- Throw away anything broken, or repair it and recycle.
- Clear out old magazines, letters, junk.
- Have a house "spring clean."
- Dig weeds out of the garden.
- Start a compost bin for raw waste foods.
- Release yourself from obligations which do not reflect your heart space.
- Look out for any negative ideas and beliefs in your workplace, family, or community.
- See how the family can help and learn more independence.
- Look at relationships, and focus on the positive ones.
- Write letters of forgiveness where there are any past hurts or resentments, and start with forgiving yourself first.
- Cut back on time spent with technology. Try a day without mobile, computer, TV, and DVD.
- Consider relinquishing the need for the car for a day or two.
- Finish any unfinished projects.

- Give yourself a "detox" day or two each week.
- Get regular exercise, plenty of water, and sleep.
- Have a pamper day, and treat yourself to all your favourite body indulgences.
- Use head, foot, hand massage each day to release brain stress.

"It's good to leave each day behind
Like flowing water, free of sadness.
Yesterday is gone and its tale told.
Today new seeds are growing."
Jelaluddin Rumi

Next Moon: The Second Secreta: Money

THE SECOND SECRETA: MONEY

Demeter really shows her understanding of the world we are living in by bringing this forward as the second teaching. Her gentle insights and suggestions help us take a fresh look at something we probably take for granted as the ongoing priority. Relax, and reflect with her as you journal.

How would you describe your relationship with money?

What was your parents' attitude to money?

How do you measure your worth?

How do you measure the worth of others?

What have you learnt along the way?

How do you share that which you have?

In what spirit do you receive when in need?

Are there areas of your life where you feel things are "warped" by the pursuit of money?

What will be your detour, your actions for free?

This Moon . . .

What a powerful call for us to search our inner selves and recognise how we truly value our own worth and that of others.

What a challenge it is to reflect on our relationship with this thing called money.

What an important facet of our values it is to consider how we share and also how we can give for free.

This month will be a time for watching how the impact of your beliefs and values on money weave their way into your life's thoughts and actions.

Like time, money is a facet of the passionate red energy of the base chakra.

It is closely linked to issues of our health, sexuality, and physical vitality and our feelings of anger, resentment, passion, freedom, and power.

If you are aware of any blockages in this energy zone, then you can help release them by taking time for the following:

- Dancing from the heart, wild and free;
- Good exercise that is fun and free and in the fresh air;
- Receiving some body/massage or chakra work to help release and rebalance your energy;
- Recognizing where there are old "wounds" that need forgiveness; and
- Visualising and meditating on the true natural abundance in your life.

Demeter needs us to be fully open to the natural abundance and beauty of the life force so that we can realise our soul potential.

Clearing away the debris from your Soul garden is of course the first step!

"Only when the last tree has died and the last river been poisoned and the last fish been caught, will we realise we cannot eat money."
Cree Indian saying

Next Moon: The Third Secreta: Soul Gardening

THE THIRD SECRETA: SOUL GARDENING

It is as if we have cleared the garden of the superficial debris so that now we can begin to dig and explore what lies underneath. What is our "soil" made of? Put your feet up with a cuppa while you contemplate on this one.

What is your personal understanding of the Soul?

Have you had personal experience of religion, doctrine, ritual, or a faith journey that has affected or restricted your relationship with your Soul?

How can you nurture your Soul with kindness, gentleness, joy, happiness, love?

What is your sense of your giftedness?

Can you describe your vision for truth?

Reflect on your wish for the world. Draw it if it helps, or use symbols on a map.

How can you contribute?

In your "Soul garden," what do you feel are the weeds?

This Moon . . .

This Secreta is so simple, yet the power of the teachings Demeter shares lead us forward to both our personal power and our responsibility.

As you practise "Soul Gardening", then journaling on a daily basis is a valuable tool.

You can record what "weeds" you find and also how you are nurturing yourself.

By the end of a month, see if you can make a list of several different ways in which you can take better care of yourself, and share it with your group or with a friend.

Spend time in stillness in your Sacred space, and honour your connectedness to the Great Mystery. Begin to vision the world you wish to create for yourself, then commit this to paper in your own tree of life drawing. This is another powerful tool for your journey.

Here are some ideas to get you started. You can add to it over the years.

My Tree of Life

- Take a big piece of paper and draw the outline of a tree.
- In the roots, write words or draw symbols that represent the values and culture of your birth family, your community, your education, your country, your world view.
- On the trunk, write a list of all the skills and things you have learnt and achieved from birth to now. (See now why you need big paper!)
- In the branches, write your personal values and beliefs.
- On the leaves, write your personal qualities, gifts, and challenges.

- On the flowers and fruits, write the things you wish to harvest, the goals you want to realise, the dreams you want to manifest.
- Above the tree, write an overall blessing for your life.
- To the left of the tree, draw the compost bin, and in there put all the things you no longer need, ready for recycling, old values, beliefs, etc.
- To the right, draw a fertilizer bin, and put in all the things you need in order to keep nurturing your growth.
- Make a list in your journal, or to stick on the fridge, of all the little things you can do daily, weekly, etc. to keep the tree growing during this year.
- Sign your drawing, roll it up, and store it safely.
- In a year, revisit your Tree of Life, and give thanks for that which has grown.
- Review your "gardening skills" and make any changes you wish for next year's harvest. Make a new list of activities for your Soul Garden.
- Repeat this process annually, and you will be surprised how powerful it is.
- After twenty-one years, you can display your Tree of Life drawing as a blessing to Yourself.

Be sure that things will start to grow from this symbolic process. It acts as a conversation with the Great Mystery and attracts new opportunities and energy into your life. These are the "seeds" of your new soul growth. It is a wonderful partnership which can bear beautiful fruits for you, your family, and your world.

> *This is how it's meant to be*
> *Your earth walk can be harmony*
> *The truth that people need to know:*
> *What you sow is what you grow*

Next Moon: The Fourth Secreta: Fragrance and Flavour

THE FOURTH SECRETA: FRAGRANCE AND FLAVOUR

ere Demeter is approaching the subtleties of our higher sensory perception. When your sense of fragrance advances, then you may also learn to sense the fragrance of friends in Spirit. It is natural to start avoiding any cosmetic, body products, or perfume with a strong fragrance, as this does mask your ability to sense the etheric fragrances. Put on a flowing gown, sense your inner beauty, and light a candle as you open to this level of beauty.

What is your hunger?

How and when do you allow yourself to sense on an inner level?

What and where is the natural fragrance in your life?

Can you appreciate your sense of flavour/appetite for life?

Which thoughts, words, and actions create the fragrance and flavours that you like?

Which seeds do you wish to plant and nurture for your future harvest?

Are there new things to learn as you become a chef for life?

Do you want a banquet or a snack?

This Moon . . .

In order to begin to develop the degree of awareness and sensitivity, which will enable you to explore this teaching for yourself, it is helpful to practise "mindfulness.'

This way of simply stopping and becoming totally "mindful" of the sensory environment, of the here and now, of this present moment and how you are feeling, is considered a meditation practise, but it can be done anywhere for a small amount of time with great effect.

In a way, it is like shining an intense spotlight on yourself for a few moments of your day.

Try catching yourself as if glancing in a mirror, in the queue at the supermarket, in the shower, after some exercise, whilst you are in the middle of the washing up, having a cup of tea, or during a journey where you do not have to drive.

Simply stop, focus, listen, smell, taste, and feel; sense the essence of you.

Then ask how you feel about the fragrance and the flavour of that point in time, that specific situation, those people around you, about yourself.

This is a doorway to the indigo of the brow chakra, which governs our intuition and insight. It is deeply connected to the roots of our creativity, which lies in the sacral, orange chakra. We cannot fully enter the creative zone unless we can appreciate, open, and respond to our inner senses.

Journaling these little "jewels of consciousness" on a daily basis will help you become more skilled and comfortable with this beautiful aspect of your Sacred self.

This writing and reflection acts as preparation for the deepening of our awareness through the next Secreta.

Mine the beauty and fragrance
Of a woman in repose
Mine the everlasting Peace
The cup that overflows
Song of Mary

Next Moon: The Fifth Secreta: Silence and Stillness

THE FIFTH SECRETA: SILENCE AND STILLNESS

If Demeter could have included this Secreta without words, then I strongly believe that she would have done so!

As she declares that she suspects it will be hard for us, so I sensed it was extremely hard for her to actually give form to this concept of "Ancient Knowing" through silence, through listening, through hearing the Song of our Soul.

However, I felt that she came back to this Secreta several times to try to make it as clear as she could for us to understand.

Even so, I find it contains concepts, which I have to truly sit with myself in order to hear the true meaning of her words.

She so desperately wants us to gather the necessary skills and tools for our journey into the garden of the Great Mystery, and yet she has a full sense of how noisy and busy life is for us today and how far we have come away from this aspect of deeper communication.

As with the earlier Secretas, I feel we have to trust her guidance as she is leading us wisely and gently to deeper self-knowledge and greater personal power.

Before you start journaling, simply sit and reflect on silence and sense:

- How does silence feel for me?
- Do I feel any resistance?
- Where and how do I feel this in my body?
- Do I sense any relief?
- Where and how do I feel this in my body?
- When I am silent, what do I hear?
- Do I avoid silence?

In your journal, draw a picture of how silence feels.

What colour is it?

What shape and texture?

What fragrance or flavour?

Does it move or change?

Take quiet time to reflect on Demeter's insights for us as she helps us connect with the power of silence as a part of sacred Life.

Have you ever heard the Song of your Soul?

How do you feel about your Inner Wisdom?

What are you sensing about the essential qualities of your Soul?

When do you get time to listen to the Song of Nature?

Do you feel you ever give yourself the chance for peace?

This Moon . . .

Practise little pockets of silence throughout this moon.

It may be easier some days than others.

Take time in your sacred space to just be.

Watch yourself for any avoidance strategies or excuses.

Write, draw, and reflect on how you feel.

Before you talk, think
Is it necessary?
Is it true?
Will it hurt anyone?
Will it improve on the silence?
Sai Baba

Next Moon: The Sixth Secreta: Being Alone

The Sixth Secreta: Being Alone

What beautiful comfort in these words.

What reassurance of our connections with Spirit, "You are **never** alone" and "This friend is ever with you".

But what a challenge for us to find this time without other people!

Or is it?

Demeter here is strong and forthright in her reasons for wanting us to make this time to be alone and find our place of "self-truth", to be open to the workings of the Great Mystery and connect with our friends in Spirit.

This brings us up to the magenta violet of the crown chakra and our connections with the Universal energy of Great Love.

Demeter certainly appreciates that we may need courage to step away from the crowd.

When you have had time to reflect on her message, then come back and journal.

What are the distractions that pull you away from your own self?

How can you organize some time just for you to be on your own?

What fears are there for you in being alone?

Have you ever sensed the presence of a friend in Spirit?

How do you feel about being authentic, about having the integrity of your own true self?

How do you find courage?

This Moon . . .

Can you rise to the challenge of creating a regular and significant space of time to be alone?

Perhaps you can get up early and go for a daily walk or swim on your own. This is a frequent time when I receive my inspirations from Spirit.

When you are ironing or doing the dishes can be a valuable alone time, if you remain mindful, as the left brain is usefully occupied with a functional task which leaves the right brain free for "receptive" insights.

Maybe your children can visit friends whilst your husband or partner is out at sport. Maybe as a special occasion, you can organize for your family to take a break without you for a day or two, leaving you at home.

Take a quiet break in the garden before bedtime, watch the moon and the stars, and wonder at the universe.

Make the focus your sense of inner truth and connection with Demeter.

Think creatively, and begin to ask for this time for yourself.

As we continue to watch and learn about ourselves, so we can begin to realise where we are compromising and conforming, not from our own heart space but from our wish to fit in, to be like everyone else, to fulfil the expectations of others.

How wonderful to begin to recognise our especial giftedness, the fruits of our own strength and beauty.

Find a special way to celebrate this with your beautiful self.

This Secreta completes the Second Triad and concludes the preparations of our "soil" in readiness for the next season of our Soul Gardening.

The First Triad laid the foundations for our introduction to learning the Secretas of the Great Mystery. This next triad has given us the tools we need to build on those foundations so that we can take control and responsibility for growing our very own, glorious tree of Life.

Demeter is gradually helping us to acquire the skills we need to use these tools, as she would have us succeed and know that we are at one with the Great Mystery.

Beyond the rim and through the veil
You may not see but still it's real
The Ancient ones stay close and care
The Land of Spirit is always there

Next Moon: The Seventh Secreta: The Power to Create and Destroy

The Seventh Secreta: The Power to Create and Destroy

From the secure foundations of the first two triads, Demeter now gets straight to the heart of her intentions for us, to understand the nature of our own Power.

She also gives such clear reasons for sharing the Secretas with us and helping us with our Soul gardening this year, that there might be a "wider benefit to humanity" from our increased understanding, and also that she does not want us to be deluded, oppressed, or living in fear.

I sense her passion here, her dedication, her compassion, and her urgency. "I have no time to waste", she declares.

She certainly speaks plainly as she challenges us to look at our reasons for doing the things that we do, making the choices which we make and complying with the laws and expectations which we allow to rule our everyday behaviours and interactions.

Her total commitment to free choice, which is beyond the structures of Law and Power in our society, brings us to a space of freedom, which is to be guided by "true preference, mature understanding, and deep vision".

This is certainly a place of enormous power and huge responsibility if we are to work with this natural "Law of Returns".

As you work with this Secreta, remember the preparation which she has already guided you through and the tools which she has already given you:

- Your relationship with time and money
- Your vision for your Tree of Life
- Your increased sensitivity to fragrance and flavour
- Your use of silence and the Song of your soul
- Your connections with Spirit when you are alone

Prepare to take this step forward, for this is as she would have you proceed, in this journey to the power, at the heart of the Great Mystery.

I suggest you read and reflect on this Secreta several times, before you journal. It is such a powerful teaching.

Reflect on your own life journey, and think of any examples where you have seen a kind word or action bring a happy return to the person who initiated it.

Now think of any examples of how negative or hurtful words or actions have returned a similar response to the person or someone close to him or her.

When you look at your own behaviour, see if you can recognise the systems of Law and Power which moulded, and influenced, your childhood.

How often do you truly contemplate the consequences of your choices, thoughts, words and actions before you use them?

Are there people whom you blame for the things which have gone wrong in your life?

How do you feel about personal responsibility?

Make two lists, one of the rubbish you find and one of the treasures. Next to each, write how you intend to use it.

This Moon . . .

Concentrate on how you make choices on contemplating the consequences before you act or speak and on watching how the law of returns operates around you.

Keep writing and reflecting.

> *I want to walk the streets with my head held high*
> *Want my kids to be safe, no more tears to cry*
> *From my heart this is a woman's plea*
> *Gonna start right now, trust the power in me*
> **Not Guilty song**

Next Moon: The Eighth Secreta: Vision Dreaming

THE EIGHTH SECRETA: VISION DREAMING

Following swiftly on from our introduction to personal power, we have another beautiful jewel of wisdom here from Demeter as she moves straight into the challenge of helping us discover and realise our dreams.

Recognising our inner desires and then harnessing our potential to create, she leads us into the energy space where we can begin to choose our "seeds" and focus our efforts for achievement and success.

You may well feel that you want to go back to your Tree of Life and add more or different "fruits" once you have mastered this art of Vision Dreaming, once you know that there are no boundaries for your vision.

You will almost certainly pause to reflect on your own broken dreams, any lack of personal fulfilment, or restricted beliefs about your own capabilities.

I find her insight into Broken Dream Syndrome challenges the established view of some of our biggest health issues in the Western world. What do you feel?

Before we journal, we need to enter this space for Vision Dreaming.

Take a Sacred time and space.

Sit gently with yourself, and let yourself relax. Close your eyes.

Let your breath flow deeper and deeper, the rhythm of the in and out breaths even and smooth.

Relax the body from head to toes.

Open your brow and crown chakras, and be ready to receive from your highest inspirational source.

Dream of your life as you vision it could be, as you wish it to be.

Hold your dream, and breathe colour, fragrance, flavour and song into it.

Feel yourself glowing with fulfilment from the heart.

Allow yourself to resonate with this sense of joy.

Feel your resonance circling out and touching others with the beauty of your Vision Dream.

When you are ready, give thanks for your vision and gently bring yourself back to this moment. Take three long, slow, deep breaths, and open your eyes.

Now, take pastels or pens and a big sheet of paper. Make a symbolic map or picture of your Vision Dream.

Next write a few words to establish the structure of your Vision Dream.

Begin to translate it into small but concrete actions.

Where will you start to plant the seed and nurture the growth of this Vision Dream so that it can fulfil you and help you achieve a successful harvest.

Have you learnt anything about your personal beliefs?

Did you discover any boundaries, any logical blocks to seeding your dream?

If so, see if you can explore where they are rooted and work to release them.

This Moon . . .

Allow yourself this time to relax and vision.

You may find yourself returning to your original Vision Dream and expanding it, or you may discover different, smaller but connected facets of your Vision.

Affirm your own power by firstly achieving a simple small wish that you hold for yourself, or initiate a bigger life creation and take steps towards it. Journal your progress and celebrate each and every little step you commit to.

With each dream,
I capture a glimpse of the Jewels
Bestowed on me since the beginning of time

Next Moon: The Ninth Secreta: The Balance of the Dark and the Light

THE NINTH SECRETA: THE BALANCE OF THE DARK AND THE LIGHT

Dear bold Demeter, what a teacher!

I embrace her determination to set things straight for us humans in our journey to understand the Great Mystery.

Proclaiming the beauty of our dark side runs against the tide of so many orthodox teachings, and yet, with her wisdom and explanations, we can finally begin to release a huge amount of fear and guilt. What a relief!

I do not know how long we have waited for the revelation of these Secretas, but I am totally overjoyed at the impact of them in my own life and in the lives of those who are also working with her this year.

Take time then to reflect on your "dark side" qualities, your mistakes in life, your "bad" choices, and then connect with the lessons you have learnt, what positive qualities you have gained as a result of something you originally believed to be "bad" or wrong.

As a woman, as a mother, can you imagine a situation, an occasion in which you might be moved to do something which is deemed wrong or illegal (e.g., killing, stealing, or destroying)?

Are there other mistakes or errors that you feel have made? What has been the outcome?

How do you feel about natural justice?

Take time to feel and appreciate the energy of the moon, in all her aspects. Feel her power in you as she moves the tides. How do you give her your attention?

What hidden aspects of yourself are clearing and coming up for healing as you work with Demeter?

Focus again on your giftedness. How is this emerging?

How are you embracing all that you are?

How do you feel about Demeter's wish to heal the world?

This Moon . . .

Try keeping a moon journal.

Follow her stages of waxing to fullness and waning to darkness again.

Watch your own energies and attune to this deeper wisdom, which affects us all on an emotional and insightful level.

Celebrate when she is full; retreat and reflect when she is dark.

Initiate new projects and consolidate with the new and waxing moon, and release old patterns as she wanes.

Each month, this energy is available to us to help us keep on flowing with our Soul journey.

Girlfriends, sisters, mothers and wives
Come together and sing of the truth in our lives
Times can be hard, pain makes us blue
But it's laughter and love that helps us pull through
Living, Laughing, Caring, Sharing for each other
Women's Song

Next Moon: The Tenth Secreta: The Great Love

THE TENTH SECRETA: THE GREAT LOVE

Here we are already at the final triad, and Demeter brings us powerfully into the full energy of the Great Mystery.

Every time I read this Secreta, it brings tears as she touches my heart with her beauty, strength, and wisdom.

You probably need to read it more than once to begin to absorb the fullness of her insights into this power of Love.

What is special for me is the way she explains so much about why she is teaching us these things. I find it always helps to understand the why!

When you are ready, sit quietly, open your heart like a rose opening to release its fragrance in the morning sunlight, and begin to reflect on her questions.

Your inner truth will flow when you are open in this heart space.

Who do you think you are now?

Is this a different you from the one who started reading at the first Secreta?

How are you feeling?

Is life any easier for you now, any simpler, any more enjoyable?

Is what you are creating that of which you dream, or are there still remnants of instilled fear?

How are you accepting that which has been created so far, that which is?

What do you think are the changes within yourself and in your life so far?

Are you ready to travel further?

Are there aspects of yourself that you are still not fully comfortable with?

Do you want to transform the destiny of your life, to come to wholeness?

Where is Love in your life?

What kind of a space do you give to it?

When and how do you feel connected to the beauty of Love?

Can you sense the freedom which love brings to help you with your giftedness?

How do you feel about spreading your wings?

Is your heart open to the way of fearlessness?

Are you beginning to understand this power of Love and the Law of Natural Returns?

Are there things you wish to change now for more Love in your life?

Find out about the Labyrinth or mandalas. Create a visual image of this symbolic inner landscape.

This Moon . . .

Watch yourself and how Love operates in your life.

Write about it, or create a work of art, when it is in flow.

Write about when it is difficult, or express it in a way that speaks without words.

Learn about when you want to give, when you feel you want to receive, when you wish to do neither.

Watch the conditions of your love. Learn about your boundaries, and challenge them. Demeter will be right there with you if you ask for her help.

Try starting the day with a blessing that opens the heart.

Dedicate your day to Love, and see what happens.

Close your day with Love, and surrender what was hard and not loving to the moon's energy for clearing during the night.

> *In the silence of my heart of hearts,*
> *I remember that I am in harmony*
> *With the wholeness of the universe*

Next Moon: The Eleventh Secreta: Inspiration, Vision, Hope

The Eleventh Secreta: Inspiration, Vision, Hope

Demeter calls this last Triad the "Golden Triangle" and to me it certainly feels like a "power pack".

After all the hard work of our Soul gardening, we begin to reach harvest, and what a joy that feels!

Again, take your time to read and understand what she is sharing here before you begin to journal.

How have you taken the Tenth Secreta of Great Love into your daily life?

Can you see the results coming in your harvest?

Do you feel there is more work that you wish to do?

How does the prospect of your own brilliance feel to you?

What hope, what vision, and what inspirations do you feel as a part of your life now?

How do these link to your wish for the world?

Do you feel comfortable now receiving the messages, the seeds planted in your heart?

This Moon . . .

Start with yourself, and practise letting Love be a regular part of your day and night.

Open to the tenderness of the heart, and allow inspiration, vision, hope to enter freely.

Find as many ways of creatively expressing this feeling as you can, or focus on just one and practise till you shine!

Trust that in allowing Great Love to flow through you, your life will begin to be enlightened.

Write, sing, dance, draw in celebration of this power that you hold, to quite simply just choose Love.

Wholly Woman
Dancing through the night
Wholly woman
Weave your web of Light

Next Moon: The Twelfth Secreta: Truth

THE TWELFTH SECRETA: TRUTH

After the last two Secretas of the heart, Demeter aims directly into the core of our being as Soul Gardeners to complete this shining lesson in Truth.

Can you feel her passion and determination?

Does it challenge you as you read it?

Take a few deep breaths, and slowly unpack what she is saying.

Go for a walk and contemplate before you begin to journal.

Do you feel like you are standing tall and aiming straight?

Are you nurturing those who struggle beside you?

Are you living in your truth?

How are you using your gifts?

How are you spending your time and money?

How do you feel when there is suffering amongst your family, friends, in your community, our world?

How are you celebrating your harvest of your own Soul Garden gifts?

How are you sharing with others?

Where is the sense of Sacred in your life?

Where is your faith?

Is there love in your heart?

Is there acceptance of your humanity?

Are you embracing every little part of you, every single grain of your Soul soil?

Do you feel the power of your truth?

This Moon . . .

You might want to create a "power statement", which you can place in your Sacred space. Let it represent the truth of who you really are now.

Maybe you can begin to plan a celebration which honours your year of learning with Demeter, which celebrates your harvest.

Share it with your circle, some special friends or family.

> *Live each day as if your last*
> *Forget the future and the past*
> *It's time for now to be at Peace*
> *Forgiveness heals and brings release*
> *Are you ready?*
> *Hear this call*
> *We are one, we are all*
> *Yes, we are one, and we are all*

Next Moon: Zenith

ZENITH

As I read this teaching from Demeter, I sense the angst which every mother feels as she watches her children prepare to leave home.

The questions uppermost in her mind of : *Have I done a good job? Will they be able to survive with the skills that I have tried to give them? Will they find a place which is safe for them to continue their growth?*

I feel Demeter is almost reluctant to let us go, as if she is really questioning herself : *Am I really ready to let them learn through the painful lessons which life may deliver? Will they be able to stay as beautiful, open-hearted individuals amidst the chaos of the world?*

These are the fears that we all share in our deepest maternal hearts as we support our children in their quest for independence, and Demeter is every bit the mother here.

She is supporting us in our growing Sacred Soul wisdom and tenderness, to realise the vital importance of the open heart in our inner garden.

If we can consider ourselves as "saplings" in the Cosmic Soul garden, then maybe we can allow ourselves to appreciate our own needs for nurturing and tenderness in our growth process at this early stage.

Demeter is inspiring us to grow into the greatness which comes from our maturity of understanding, the focus of our insight and inspiration, the patience, courage, and determination of true, "Soul Gardeners".

In this way, we help to fulfil her vision for the creation of a better world, "for the advancement of the whole human race".

If we truly want to see change, then we must proceed with open hearts from the wisdom of our Sacred Space as we claim this duality of power and responsibility.

We can now see the truth of her statement at the beginning of the manuscript, that our lives will never be the same again.

Take your time as you absorb her passion here and her love for you as one of her saplings.

Before you write and reflect in your Journal, survey your own inner landscape.

Reflect carefully on the questions she poses before you answer.

Do you feel comfortable with the impact of the Law of Natural Returns?

Which parts of your growth do you like?

Where do you need to be gentle and forgiving with yourself?

What do you see as "wilderness", as the chaos in the world, and how does this affect you?

Are you feeling happy and comfortable with your own Sacred space?

How have you experienced the opening and closing of the heart energy?

What strategies can you use when you feel vulnerable?

Do you feel inspired to "shine" as an example of the work you have done with Demeter?

This Moon . . .

Review all the tools which Demeter has given you; see which ones you feel you are skilled with and which ones still need more practise.

Try writing or mapping a summary of your year.

Focus on your tenderness to yourself when there is a feeling of chaos or uncertainty.

This Earth is Sacred
Believe in Love
Release all hatred
Breathe in Love

Next moon: Epilogue

EPILOGUE

Demeter gives us what feels like her final blessing as she releases us to keep seeding, and bearing, the "fruits" which we have chosen.

The strength of her teaching on the need to be clear in our intentions, desires, thoughts, and actions reminds us of the power we all hold to create a "bigger harvest for the World".

As she has offered to us, so we are empowered to share with others.

From what we have gained, in our personal wisdom of her teachings, to the effects they have had on our lives, we stand as her "harvest". the "cream of the crop" born from the Great Mystery.

Reflect on your whole life journey so far, choose the seeds and fruits for the coming year, and prepare to begin the cycle of growth to create your own harvest of rewards all over again!

What I bring is stillness,
What I share is Love.
The Secret of my Healing Ways
Soothes the Soul,
Bringing strength for each new day

My Vision Dream for Next Year

Start with a blank canvas and vision your beauty . . .

THE CLOSING

The Song of Aphrodite

I am the dream between lovers,

I am the fresh breeze from the sea,

I am the gentle whisper through the trees,

I am the playful dance in the mountain streams,

I am the warm stroke of the morning sun,

I am the soft caress of the summer rain,

I am the sweet fragrance under the evening sky,

I am the first starlight on a dark night,

I am the *ease* in release,

I am the silent Song of your Soul,

I am the Mother of Love.

Welcome home.

A blessing given to Tricia in Cyprus, the birthplace of the Goddess Aphrodite, in 2010.

References for *The Demeter Story*

Eleusis: The Eleusian Mysteries: George E. Mylonas: Princeton University Press: 1961, New Jersey, United States.

Greek and Egyptian Mythologies: Yves Bonnefoy: University of Chicago Press: 1991-1992, Chicago, United States.

Greek Popular Religion: Martin P Nilsson: Columbia University Press: 1940, Massachusetts, United States.

Encyclopedia of World Mythology: Peerage Books: 1983: London, United Kingdom.

ABOUT THE AUTHOR AND SCRIBE

Tricia Mary Lee considers herself to be a woman of many blessings.

She is a daughter, sister, mother of two sons, wife, aunty, niece, and girlfriend.

Her work and life experiences have taken her from being a teacher for young special-needs children in England to being a consultant to the Kimberley Literacy Project in remote areas of Western Australia. Trained as a professional Reflexologist in England, just prior to her *big move* to Australia, her journey to healing gathered momentum at the age of 39. From practising and training others in the techniques of Reflexology and natural health, this has now evolved into her work with volunteers, focussing on the importance of touch therapy for the elderly and terminally ill.

The journey to writing and being a scribe has grown naturally from a love of creative experession and journaling and this now features as an important part of her everyday life and work.

She is also a Celebrant, creating meaningful marriage ceremonies and promoting the role of personal ceremony and ritual for life's events, both great and small.

For fun, she loves the richness of the visual and performing arts, being a singer/dancer/choreographer, and working with her local theatre group.

The special and most important part of any of these experiences is sharing, caring, and celebrating with others in her community.

Her work with Sacred Circles of women weaves through the many colours and facets of her life's experience and wisdom.

She says, "My love for life is my spiritual practise. My family, my friends, and this beautiful Earth around me are my teachers."

She confesses to a wild gypsy streak and loves to travel, welcoming learning, change, and growth as vital facets of her dynamic feminine soul.

She currently lives, works, and plays in her *garden* of the majestic Southern Forest region and the south-west coastal areas of Australia. She also makes regular visits back to her much-loved family in Yorkshire and her Celtic homeland of England.

She enjoys sharing her passion for Sacred life through circle work, talks, workshops, conferences and retreats. She also visits community groups, schools, and children's groups with her cosmic fairy tale, "The Star Who Lost Her Sparkle", promoting natural health, well-being, and delight in our beautiful planet, Earth.

The below publications are available by personal order from Tricia Mary at tricialee1@mac.com.

For Women

Stop Punishing Yourself
Wise Women Words
The Ishtar Manuscript: Jewels of the Night
The Mary Manuscript: Lessons for a Pure and Blessed Life
The Ceridwen Manuscript: The Book of Ceremonies
The Art of Transcendence: Almeera

For Children

The Star Who Lost Her Sparkle (Published by Pick a Woo-woo)

"Through these words,
I release my Great Love
for this beautiful Planet Earth
and all her people."
Demeter